MARY OF NAZARETH,
✳   ✳   ✳   ✳   ✳   ✳
PROPHET OF PEACE

JOHN DEAR
Foreword by Joan Chittister, O.S.B.

© 2003 by Ave Maria Press, Inc.

www.avemariapress.com

International Standard Book Number: 0-87793-982-9

Icons by William Hart McNichols

Cover and text design by Katherine Robinson Coleman

Printed and bound in the United States of America.

Library of Congress Cataloging-in-Publication Data
Dear, John, 1959-
Mary of Nazareth, prophet of peace / John Dear.
    p. cm.
ISBN 0-87793-982-9 (pbk.)
1. Mary, Blessed Virgin, Saint. I. Title.

BT603 .D43 2003
232.91--dc21

                                    2003000326
                                    CIP

For Sr. Helen Prejean, C.S.J.

and Sr. Margaret Maggio, C.S.J.,

Friends and Peacemakers

Contents

Be thou then, O thou dear Mother, my
    atmosphere;

My happier world, wherein to wend and
    meet no sin;

Above me, round me lie, fronting my
    forward eye

With sweet and scarless sky; Stir in my ears,
    speak there

Of God's love, O live air, of patience,
    penance, prayer;

World-mothering air, air wild,

Wound with thee, in thee is led,

Fold home, fast fold thy child.

Gerard Manley Hopkins

Mary ever Virgin, Mother of God our Savior, I entrust myself entirely to your loving intercession and care because you are my Mother and I am your child, full of trouble, conflict, error, confusion and prone to sin. My whole life must change, but because I can do nothing to change it by my own powers, I entrust it with all my needs and cares to you. Present me with pure hands to your Divine Son. Pray that I may gladly accept all that is needed to strip me of myself and become his true disciple, forgetting myself and loving his reign, his truth, and all whom he came to save by his holy cross. Amen.

Thomas Merton

Mary Most Holy, Mother of All Nations, help us recall that the universe is one song of praise, and we are all created to be the beloved of God. Make us all one in the Trinity. All nations. No Nations. No boundaries, only expanses. No borders, only homelands. No separations, only communion. As it was in the beginning. Amen.

Megan McKenna

Acknowledgments

I would like to thank Sr. Carolyn Capuano and the Sisters of the Humility of Mary at Villa Maria, Pennsylvania, for inviting me to offer these reflections at their Advent Retreat in December 2001. That invitation and their warm hospitality stirred me to put this book together.

Next I would like to thank Jack McSherry, S.J., for helping me with the manuscript, for his comments, editing, and encouragement.

Then, I want to thank all those who supported me while I wrote this book, my friends at the West Side Jesuit Comminity in New York City; my parents; Mary Donnelly and Lyn Reale on Block Island; and Dar Williams, Patty Smythe, Lynn Fredriksson, Kathy Kelly, Mary Anne Muller, Mairead Maguire, Megan McKenna, and Shelley and Jim Douglass.

Thanks, also, to Bill McNichols for the use of his magnificent icons. I hope readers will go to his website found on the copyright page for more wonderful icons. They are beautiful reminders of our Christian life.

Since I wrote this book, I have moved to New Mexico where I am the pastor of several churches out in the desert and in the mountains. So I offer this as a gift with gratitude to my new friends and parishioners in Cimarron, Springer, Maxwell, Eagle Nest, Tinaja, Palo Blaco, Black Lake, and Angel Fire.

Finally, my special thanks to Joan Chittister for her foreword, her friendship, and her great witness; and to Daniel Driscoll and Ave Maria Press for bringing this little book to the light of day.

I dedicate this book to two of my heroes and friends, Helen Prejean and Margaret Maggio, who have carried on the example of Mary as contemplatives, activists, and prophets of peace. Thank you both, and may the God of peace bless you always.

Foreword

An ancient Chinese proverb teaches, "There is my truth, your truth, and the truth." The message is clear: Where we stand determines what we see, and none of us sees all of it at one time. Worse, sometimes nearsighted or blinded by the glare of the self, we lose the little perspective we have.

As children of a global world, ironically, our vision is even more limited than ever before. When we lived in small villages, we knew every path, every person, every possible array of options and opportunities in the place. We knew our place in our small local universe. We understood the needs of the others around us because their challenges and burdens, their obstacles and impossibilities were our own.

But things have changed. Our world has expanded but our vision has not. For us in the U.S., our parochialism betrays us. Most of us have never been out of the United States of America. We are still only beginning to get accustomed to the differences right in our midst, let alone in the wider world around us. We are still getting accustomed to the integration of Protestants and Catholics, of black and white, of male and female. And even those tentative associations are full of uncertainty, of tension. Even here, we are yet strangers to one another.

The rest of the world is at best a blur or a fantasy to Americans. We can't imagine why they aren't like us. We can't conceive why they just don't work harder so they can have what we have. We can't see why their governments aren't democracies. We wonder why they hate us. But we have not seen abject poverty. We have not lived with the drought and famine that industrialism in other parts of the world can cause. We do not know what it must be like to find death more desirable than life. We do not understand desperation. What's worse, we have been brought up on playground politics: If they hit you, hit them back. Or even more terrible, hit them before they hit you.

"Might makes right" is the real national anthem of a country with the power to impose it.

After years of Cold War, after decades of fear, after scores of treaties signed and treaties broken, after the global sigh of relief that came with the demise of the Soviet Union, the unthinkable has happened. Nuclear retaliation has been mentioned with seriousness as a possible U.S. strategy against aggression, and a Gallup Poll of public opinion released in December 2002 finds that over two-thirds of the U.S. population approve of the first use of nuclear weapons in recrimination for assault. We have entered the madness of power in defiance of the theology of peace. "The release of the power of the atom has changed everything except our way of thinking," Albert Einstein wrote. "Thus we drift toward a catastrophe of unparalleled magnitude." Where as a people can we possibly go to cure such insanity? Where is Christianity in times such as these? Who are our heroes now? Who must be our guides in this darkness, the government or the gospel?

John Dear answers these questions for us. He takes us into the heart and life of Mary, the Mother of Jesus. An unmarried woman in a society highly controlling of women, Mary faces down every system—nonviolently, but clearly nonetheless—to give birth to the Christ. And she prevails. In the face of condemnation by both synagogue and society, Mary, the peacemaker, transcends the pressures of social norms and violent reprisals to bring us the Life of the world. And when the life of the world is threatened again, today, here, Mary, the peacemaker, has something to say to us again about what it means to be a person of God in godless times.

We have clearly strayed from the Mount of the Beatitudes. But *Mary of Nazareth, Prophet of Peace* takes us back to our roots. It is a troubling little book. That's why it must be read. Survival of the planet may depend on it. Or, as Abraham Heschel put it, "Our concern is not how to worship in the catacombs but how to stay human in the skyscrapers."

—*Joan Chittister,* O.S.B.

Introduction

This little book was born in New York City during the turbulent months at the end of 2001. Earlier that year, I had been invited to lead a retreat for the first weekend in Advent, in December 2001, for over one hundred sisters and friends at the headquarters of the Sisters of the Humility of Mary in Villa Maria, Pennsylvania. I knew that I wanted to speak of Advent as a time to prepare for the coming of the God of peace, as a season of prayer, hope and nonviolence. But I was not sure how to invite this active Christian community deeper into familiar Advent themes.

On the morning of September 11, 2001, I was having breakfast with my parents in their hotel room overlooking Central Park in Manhattan when we heard the news that an airplane had just crashed into the World Trade Center. They left town immediately, and I began to volunteer as a chaplain for the Red Cross.

Within a few days, I was asked to be a supervisor for the chaplain program, working with over five hundred chaplains at the Family Assistance Center in mid-town Manhattan. In the weeks that followed, I met with and consoled some 1,500 relatives who lost loved ones in the disaster, as well as hundreds of rescue workers, firefighters and police officers at Ground Zero.

At the same time, I spoke out against the U.S. bombing of Afghanistan at rallies and conferences in New York City and around the country. My friends and I walked in marches, held anti-war banners at vigils, sang at prayer services, and were even arrested for nonviolent civil disobedience at the U.S. mission to the United Nations, in each case denouncing war, and calling for peace and nonviolent alternatives.

As those intense weeks unfolded and the Advent retreat loomed, I found myself struggling to fulfill two biblical commandments: to love my neighbors and to love my enemies. I was feebly trying to do what Jesus would do and would want me to do. I wanted to show compassion to everyone who suffered in New York City that day, as well as to the people of Afghanistan, Iraq, and Palestine. I wanted to practice Jesus' compassion, extending to every human being on the planet, especially to the poor, the marginalized, and the ostracized.

During those days, I found in Mary's story a shining example of the journey to the peace of God. Her story showed me the basic steps on the road to peace, from contemplative nonviolence to active nonviolence to prophetic nonviolence. Before examining those three movements of the spiritual life in this meditation, I want to reflect on the world of violence, the alternative of nonviolence, and God's essential nature of peace.

The World of Violence

The months following September 11th were filled with grief. Like all New Yorkers, I mourned the loss of life at the World Trade Center and tried to console countless parents, spouses, and children. But I also mourned the ongoing loss of life in Afghanistan, Palestine, and Iraq, where over one million people have died from U.S. sanctions on Iraq since 1990.

For years, I have struggled to promote peace. The work of peace, I have learned bitterly, requires entering the grief, powerlessness and helplessness of the millions who suffer from war and poverty, and from that painful vantage point, calling for justice and peace.

Everywhere on the planet, from New York to Kabul to Bethlehem to Baghdad to Bogata, people feel the pain of war, poverty, injustice, and terrorism. When violence hits home, most people hit back, fanning the flames of violence. War and the suffering it creates have become the primary experience for most people on the planet.

For thousands of years, we have waged war with all our hearts and energy. Most people believe that responding to violence with retaliatory violence is natural. But I believe generations of violence have left us addicted to violence and war. Today we can barely imagine another way to respond to violence, much less a future world without war.

More than thirty-five wars are currently being fought, while over 50,000 people, mostly children, die every day of starvation, according to the United Nations. Tens of thousands of nuclear weapons still exist without any serious international movement toward disarmament while the environment itself continues to be destroyed. The insanity of violence, bombs, terrorism, war, poverty, nuclear weapons, greed, hunger, and environmental degradation has brought us to the brink of global disaster. We are currently in the midst of a full scale catastrophe. September 11th was just the latest sign of the depth of our predicament.

The history of war has proved that violence is not just immoral and illegal, but downright impractical. It simply does not work. It cannot solve our problems. It only foments further problems down the road. It leaves a trail of blood, bodies, tears, and resentment. Violence in response to violence can only lead to further violence.

The great lesson of the twentieth century is that war has not resolved our problems and brought us peace. It has only led to greater militarism and more war. This destructive behavior cannot go on forever. At some point, the world will break. This is our future if our present course continues.

The Alternative of Nonviolence

The culture of violence has taught us to believe that there are only two responses to violence: do nothing or fight back. The great gift of Jesus and the peacemakers who followed him, from St. Francis of Assisi to Dorothy Day, is that there is a third way, the alternative of creative nonviolence.

Nonviolence is active love that seeks justice and peace for the whole human race, beginning with the poor and oppressed. It is the all-encompassing love that embraces every human being on the planet, refuses to kill anyone, and works for social justice for everyone. It leads us to dismantle every weapon of violence, from the nuclear bomb to the handgun.

Nonviolence recognizes every human being as an equal sister and brother, a child of God. From this vision of the heart, nonviolence leads us to renounce violence and work tirelessly for an end to war and poverty. It does not require the taking of life, but the giving of one's life for suffering humanity. It demands sacrifice, commitment, creativity, struggle, and persistent reconciliation. Because it disrupts our lives and requires risks by us on behalf of others and the truth of peace, it hurts. It is costly. While it is certainly a political tactic and strategy for social change, nonviolence is essentially a way of life. It is a living prayer for the coming of God's reign of peace, and so, a life of permanent resistance to the world's wars and injustices.

Nonviolence always rejects war as an option, no matter how desperate the situation or noble the cause. It insists there is no just war. It believes that we were created to live at peace with one another, that we must promote social justice for the poor and marginalized, and that a new non-military culture is possible. When nonviolence is taught, practiced, and organized as a social movement against injustice and imperialism, it can lead to the peaceful transformation of entire societies. Indeed, given the full commitment of its practitioners, including a willingness to suffer imprisonment and death, nonviolence guarantees such peaceful change.

Gandhi's nonviolence peacefully brought independence to India. Martin Luther King Jr.'s nonviolence led to the end of segregation in the United States. The People Power nonviolence in the Philippines brought down the Marcos dictatorship in a matter of three days. Organized nonviolence in Norway, Denmark, and Bulgaria stopped Nazi violence in its tracks. There are hundreds of examples of transforming, revolutionary nonviolence taking on tyranny, injustice, and oppression, opening up new possibilities for peace and justice. (For further reading, see *A Force More Powerful* by Peter Ackerman and Jack Duvall, and *Protest, Power and Change*, edited by Roger Power and William Vogele.)

Nonviolence works on every level, from the international to the interpersonal. If we study and practice nonviolence, we can learn to respond to threats against us personally with an instinctive nonviolent response. Instead of hurting a mugger, we will be able to disarm him nonviolently. We will develop self-defense methods that do not kill either the mugger or the enemy of our nation. As Gandhi dreamed, we will create international peacemaking teams that can respond to global hot-spots by sending in thousands of trained, unarmed peacemakers to disarm conflict.

"The essence of nonviolence is love," the Buddhist monk Thich Nhat Hanh writes. "Out of love and the willingness to act selflessly, strategies, tactics, and techniques for a nonviolent struggle arise naturally. Nonviolence is not a dogma; it is a process. Other struggles may be fueled by greed, fear or ignorance, but a nonviolent one cannot use such blind sources of energy, for they will destroy those involved and also the struggle itself. Nonviolent action, born of the awareness of suffering and nurtured by love, is the most effective way to confront adversity."

From the perspective of nonviolence, military retaliation only inflames those who plot terrorism. The alternative of nonviolence proposes a wide array of immediate non-military steps that can address the root causes of terrorism and lead to a more lasting peace with justice for all. But it is the work of lifetime. We have to change the entire direction of our country, if we want to move from a culture of violence to a culture of nonviolence.

The United States should immediately begin dismantling every nuclear weapon and weapon of mass destruction; feed every child and refugee on the planet; fund new nonviolent, non-military international peacemaking projects; end poverty, the arms trade, unjust globalization, the death penalty, the Third World debt, and the destruction of the environment; fund AIDS medication for everyone in need in the world; and close such training camps as the School of the Americas. We should try to win over the world with love and show compassion toward everyone. In this way, we eliminate the roots of terrorism.

Christian nonviolence holds not just that war never works, or that war never leads to peace. It declares that war is not the will of God, that war has no place in the life of God, that war does not glorify God. It requires a concerted lifelong pursuit of peace that calls for nothing less than the conversion of the human race to God. What's more, it proclaims that God is not a god of war, but a God of peace. This may be the most radical breakthrough of Christianity. If Christians began to worship and obey the God of peace whom they profess, everything would change for the better.

The God of Peace and Nonviolence

The gospel proclaims that the God revealed by Jesus is a God of peace, that Jesus renounced violence, and that he embodied creative nonviolence even to the point of suffering execution at the hands of the Roman empire. As he died, he forgave those who killed him, and surrendered his soul to the God of peace. He told us to love one another, to love our enemies, to practice the all-encompassing compassion of God, and to seek God's reign of justice. He consistently taught that love is stronger than hate, that nonviolence is stronger than violence, and that life is stronger than death. After his death, the God of peace raised him up and invited us to receive his gift of peace. The risen Jesus sends us forth today to undertake his same journey.

Nonviolence is the hallmark of the gospel. Unfortunately, it is too often rejected by Christians. When the Roman empire took over the Christian movement in the third century and welcomed Christians into its military ranks, church leaders began to justify their complicity with imperial violence by drafting what eventually became the Just War Theory. St. Augustine even wrote that we could love our enemy by killing him. The Christian community quickly drifted away from the ethics of the crucified Jesus.

That same complicity with imperial violence and justification of war continues today. But though we stand on the brink of global destruction, the gospel call to creative nonviolence remains our only hope.

Jesus offers a realistic way back from the brink. He calls us to practice nonviolence on every level in our lives, from within our hearts to our behavior toward our neighbors to our policies toward the whole human race. If we want to offer future generations a world of peace, humanity has to change the way nations behave and start creating new cultures rooted in justice and reconciliation. From this gospel hermeneutic, life makes sense. If we disarmed ourselves, fed the hungry, and cared for one another, as the gospel envisions, the world would become a marvelous haven of peace for all people. Children would no longer suffer or live in fear. The God of peace would feel at home here on earth as God does in heaven.

Mary of Nazareth, Teacher of Nonviolence

With these thoughts in mind, I prepared for the Advent retreat at Villa Maria. After counseling relatives of the World Trade Center attacks during the day, I went home to the West Side Jesuit Community, opened the gospel and read about Mary's response to God.

In these classic Christian stories of the Annunciation, the Visitation, and the Magnificat, I discovered three basic movements of the spiritual life, from contemplative nonviolence to active nonviolence to prophetic nonviolence. In Mary's journey, we see the basic steps on the road to peace. When taken as a whole, the Annunciation, the Visitation, and the Magnificat (Luke 1:26-55) show how Mary became a peacemaker to our world.

Through her contemplative nonviolence she welcomed the God of peace into her life and the world. Through her active nonviolence she reached out to a person in need and loved her neighbor. Through her prophetic nonviolence she publicly announced God's reign of justice for the poor and God's mercy at work throughout history. Through her example, Mary teaches us how to be peacemakers by becoming people of contemplative nonviolence who practice active, and ultimately prophetic, nonviolence.

The Gospel of Luke leads one to assume that Jesus learned nonviolence from his mother. Just as Mary taught Jesus to worship the God of peace, to be at peace with everyone, and to proclaim God's reign of peace to a war-making world, Mary calls us to become people of peace.

This little book looks at these three aspects of Mary's journey on the road to peace in the hope that we too will take up that journey, deepen our nonviolence, worship the God of peace, love our neighbors and our enemies, and proclaim God's reign of peace and justice.

May this meditation on Mary of Nazareth, prophet of peace, help us become prophets of peace also.

John Dear

I. THE ANNUNCIATION: MARY AND CONTEMPLATIVE NONVIOLENCE

In the sixth month the angel Gabriel was sent by God to a town in Galilee called Nazareth, to a virgin engaged to a man whose name was Joseph, of the house of David. The virgin's name was Mary. And he came to her and said, "Greetings, favored one! God is with you." But she was much perplexed by his words and pondered what sort of greeting this might be. The angel said to her, "Do not be afraid, Mary, for you have found favor with God. And now, you will conceive in your womb and bear a son, and you will name him Jesus. He will be great, and will be called the Son of the Most High, and God will give to him the throne of his ancestor David. He will reign over the house of Jacob forever, and of his reign there will be no end." Mary said to the angel, "How can this be, since I am a virgin?" The angel said to her, "The Holy Spirit will come upon you, and the power of the Most High will overshadow you; therefore the child to be born will be holy; he will be called Son of God. And now, your relative Elizabeth in her old age has also conceived a son; and this is the sixth month for her who was said to be barren. For nothing will be impossible with God." Then Mary said, "Behold, I am the servant of God; let it be with me according to your word." Then the angel departed from her.

Luke 1:26-38

ONE

The Prayer of Peace

The life of peace begins with prayer. If we want peace within us, we have to sit quietly for some time each day breathing in the Holy Spirit of peace, breathing out our inner wars, handing over our inner turmoil to God, waiting to receive the gift of peace from God and attending to God's movement, voice and presence.

The story of Mary begins with Mary at prayer. In the Annunciation, we are told that six months after the angel visited Elizabeth with the astonishing news of her pregnancy, an angel visited a young woman engaged to a man named Joseph of the house of David. Mary is alone when the angel appears. She sits in solitude, in silent prayer, listening attentively for the voice of God. When the angel suddenly stands before her, he addresses her as God's favored one.

"God is with you," the angel tells Mary. "You have found favor with God," he says again, as if he himself is amazed.

Mary was a poor, young, unwed, Jewish woman living in the small village of Nazareth on the outskirts of the brutal Roman empire. She would have been familiar with poverty, oppression, sexism, humiliation, violence, hunger, militarism, terrorism, and war. Historians tell us that the Romans executed thousands of revolutionaries throughout Palestine during her lifetime. Mary might have even witnessed crucifixion firsthand, long before Jesus went to Jerusalem. According to the Roman historian Josephus, at the turn of the century, a rebel assault on the local Roman military barracks in the village of Sepphoris—just six miles from Nazareth—led the Romans to crucify over two thousand men along the road from town. Everyone would have known about it, if they did not actually suffer the loss of their loved ones to this repression.

Mary would have also been familiar with scripture, faith, hope, love, and compassion. She would have been comfortable in the search for God. After years of quiet prayer, I think Mary would have fallen in love with God.

In this world of violence, Mary retreated to her inner room and surrendered herself to the God of nonviolence. She practiced contemplative nonviolence. She was a woman of solitude, a woman of prayer, a woman of peace, a woman of nonviolence.

In the image of the Annunciation, Mary sits waiting for God and God's direction for her. She would have spent years, perhaps since she was a child, praying in peace and quiet, enjoying solitude, pondering the beauty and mystery of God. Over the years, she grew to understand herself as the servant of the God of peace. When the angel Gabriel appeared with extraordinary news, Mary responded naturally, calmly, peacefully, "Behold, I am the servant of God; let it be with me according to your word." She answered this way because she was a woman of prayer, devoted solely to the God of peace. Mary was willing to do whatever God wanted her to do.

So Mary teaches us that the first step on the road to peace is to become people of contemplative nonviolence. That means, like Mary, we need to sit in solitude and listen for God. It means giving God our violence, brokenness, anger, pain, bitterness, resentments, helplessness, and powerlessness. It means allowing God to disarm our hearts, give us the gift of peace, and send us forth into the war-making world on a peacemaking mission.

The contemplative nonviolence of Mary invites us first to be nonviolent toward ourselves and God. Mary took time in her quiet intimate prayer to make peace with herself and with God.

27

She certainly was at peace within herself because of her remarkable self-understanding as God's servant. On various occasions later on in the gospels we read that Mary pondered various experiences "in her heart." She was a reflective person; in other words, a contemplative.

Contemplative nonviolence begins as we face the violence within us. It requires that we declare a cease-fire, place our inner violence before our God, reconcile the conflicting sides within us, and make peace with ourselves. It is a daily project that we must undertake for the rest of our lives. Inner peace comes as we make peace with God more and more each day. God is already at peace with us, already loving us, blessing us, inviting us to God's reign of love. We are the ones who have rejected God's gift of peace over and over again. It is our responsibility to repent of our violence, and return to God. We need to do this privately in our own hearts and publicly in our war-making world. This heartfelt contemplative nonviolence brings peace to us and, through us, to the world. It bears good fruit, the fruit of peace that lasts forever.

Peace begins with prayer. In a world of rampant injustice, war and nuclear weapons, it is no news that there is little authentic prayer. Who has time to pray? Who believes in the power of prayer? Who cares about God? Who wants to enter the discipline, dryness, emptiness, even humiliation of prayer?

For me, prayer is quiet, daily meditation that leads to intimate love and adoration of God. It requires quality time each day, usually in a specific place of solitude and silence. In that quiet space, we turn to our God and develop an intimate, loving relationship with God. Over time, as we search for the presence of God in our lives and in our quiet prayer, God eventually touches us and our relationship deepens. Prayer then becomes quality time for intimacy with God. It is the setting for our relationship with God, which is the primary relationship for our lives.

In contemplative prayer, we sit like Mary, waiting for God. Sooner or later, God will find favor with us too, come to us, love us, and send us on a mission of love into the world.

Through our contemplative prayer, we get to know what God is like because we experience the presence of God. What does the presence of God feel like? Spiritual writers have been trying to describe the mystical experience of God for generations, and have been unable to do so adequately. They all use words such as "consolation," "peace," "love," "transformation," and "joy."

The lifelong practice of contemplative prayer leads to a profound desire to be with God. When God's presence is no longer felt, we remain content as we wait for God to return. We have fallen in love with God. God has become the primary focus of our lives. Over time the absence of consolation and joy are accepted. The quiet waiting for God is enough. This spiritual contemplative waiting breeds inner peace. Attentive prayer leads to the quiet life lived in the Spirit of peace itself.

Over time, as we sit in the presence of God and read the gospels, this contemplative prayer leads us to the realization that God is a God of love, a God of peace, a God of nonviolence. Our sinful, selfish, violent nature stands in sharp contrast to God's peace. In the light of God's compassionate love, we see our own violence, hatred, resentment, and anger with greater, shocking clarity. We pray then to be filled with God's peace.

Contemplative prayer leads us to want to share God's peace. Eventually it can heal us of our violence, brokenness, and resentment. As we sit with God and become aware of our inner violence, we beg God to disarm us and make us compassionate like God.

A Jesuit friend once told me that when he prays, he imagines sitting beside Jesus along with the person whom my friend hates the most. As he sits there in his contemplative prayer, my friend watches how Jesus looks upon his "enemy." He sees Jesus looking with the eyes of compassion upon him. This divine compassion has the effect of disarming both my friend and the one he hates. My friend learns then how to look upon him by imitating how Jesus looks upon him. With each meditation, he learns to live in a spirit of peace, freed from anger and resentment, filled with love and compassion. Each day, his heart is disarmed anew, and he is better able to do God's work of disarmament.

I recommend the following exercise as a way to develop contemplative nonviolence. Each morning, take thirty to sixty minutes sitting in silent meditation. Light a candle, read a scripture verse, and offer an opening prayer for God's blessing upon you and the world. Then, place yourself before Jesus or God as you imagine the gentle, loving God. Call to mind the person toward whom you hold a deep grudge, whoever stirs up feelings of anger, resentment, bitterness, or hatred. For some of us, there may be a long list of people who cause such feelings. We feel hurt by them, angry toward them, and bitter and resentful. Just pick one person. Tell Jesus about your anger, hatred, violence and resentment toward that person. Give those feelings to Jesus. Watch Jesus as he interacts with that person. Notice how he looks on that person with compassion, love, kindness, and truth. Why does Jesus show such deep compassion and kindness? Because that is the nature of God. Jesus is the love of God personified. He is the face of the God of nonviolence. He only knows compassion and nonviolent love. No matter how much violence, anger, resentment, or hatred we send his way, Jesus always responds with loving kindness, forgiveness, nonviolence, and compassion. In the process, he transforms us all. He saves us from our violence.

The experience of watching Jesus show compassion to the people we hate is disarming. We will feel waves of compassion come over us. Inevitably, Jesus will turn toward us with the same compassion. That spirit will overflow from within us and lead us toward a new spirit of understanding and compassion toward the person who originally stirred up such negativity within us. This exercise teaches us not so much about the other person's problems, but our own need for healing, peace, love, and God. At the heart of the whole process of peace stands Jesus loving us, showing compassion to us, drawing us into his peace.

This simple meditation disarms us, heals us, fills us with peace, and helps us to love one another. It enables us to radiate God's own peace. Through Jesus' kindness we learn not only how to love others, but first how to love ourselves, forgive ourselves, accept ourselves, and be merciful toward ourselves. His compassion touches every part of us. There is no way we can show compassion to the world if we do not show compassion to ourselves first. But if we sit with God, allow God to disarm us and love through us, we will be ready when an angel shows up with a mission for us. We will be prepared to reach out with compassion toward those in need and to speak a healing word to our broken world.

"Contemplation is simple openness to God at every moment, and deep peace," Thomas Merton wrote shortly before his death. "It means a deep realization in the very depths of our being that God has chosen and loved us from all eternity, that we really are God's children, that we really are loved by God, that there really is a personal bond and that God really is present."

"In the last few months one has often heard the complaint that the many prayers for peace are still without effect," Edith Stein wrote shortly before she was hauled away to her death in Auschwitz. "What right have we to be heard? Our desire for peace is undoubtedly genuine and sincere. But does it come from a completely purified heart? Have we truly prayed 'in the name of Jesus,' that is, not just with the name of Jesus on our lips, but with the spirit and in the mind of Jesus, for the glory of the Father alone, without any self-seeking?"

Mary calls us to prayer of the heart, to the contemplative nonviolence that springs from a pure heart. Her way of prayer leads us to peace with God and to God's will for our lives, God's mission for us, God's invitation to journey along the road to peace.

As we grow in inner peace, we can become better servants of God. We will learn to wait for God, welcome God, be filled with God's peace, radiate God's peace, and go forward on God's mission of peace. Like Mary, we will become peacemakers sent forth into the world of violence.

TWO

The Encounter with God

Rabbi Abraham Heschel once said that the whole point of prayer is not prayer per se: it's God. Our goal is not the spiritual life; it's God. Mary prayed not for the sake of being alone with herself but because she was in love with God. She wanted to be with God. She surrendered herself completely to God. She gave herself exclusively to God. She wanted to do God's will, not her own. She was God's servant, and sat in rapt attention waiting for God's direction.

Mary's encounter with the angel of God, as Raymond Brown points out, parallels Elizabeth's encounter with the angel of God, except that Mary's story surpasses Elizabeth's. In both cases, God does not intervene in Rome among the imperial military elite or in Jerusalem among the religious elite, but among poor country women, one an elderly barren woman, the other a young unwed woman. God comes to two poor women on the margins of an empire, and God's arrival through an imposing angel is not at all expected.

The greeting by the angel Gabriel stuns Mary who is much perplexed, deeply perturbed, very upset. In other words, she is scared to death. She does not know what this greeting means.

The angel senses Mary's fear and immediately tries to calm her down. "Do not be afraid, Mary," he says, "for you have found favor with God."

Mary's encounter with God is first of all terrifying. Authentic spiritual experiences are often profoundly unsettling, but if one stays with the feeling of God's presence, one soon feels the affirmation and encouragement of God's love. Because the presence of God is so startling, it frightens us. But if we dare to open ourselves to God, we need to open ourselves to the Unknown, to fear. If we wish to enter into the contemplative nonviolence modeled by Mary, we need to sit with whatever terrifies us, with our insecurities, the possibilities of change, the nightmares of the world, and the reality of death itself. If we can accept and befriend our fears, if we can sit with them, with ourselves, we will disarm them and find inner peace.

"Do not be afraid," the angel reassures Mary. This great charge is perhaps the most often repeated commandment of Jesus in all four gospels. The disciples constantly find themselves scared by Jesus' words, deeds, and miracles, whether he is walking across the water or telling them about the cross. They are afraid, but he is not, so he reassures them. We too need to hear his words of comfort. We need to heed the words of the angel and the words of Jesus, telling us not to be afraid, if we want to embark on the road to peace.

Next, the angel announces astonishing news. "You will conceive in your womb and bear a son, and you will name him Jesus. He will be great and be called Son of the Most High, and God will give him the throne of his ancestor David. He will reign over the house of Jacob forever, and of his reign, there will be no end."

What a proclamation! Who could believe such a statement, much less imagine the appearance of an angel? Mary is told that dramatic, cosmic, even salvific events will happen to her: she will conceive; she will bear a son; she will name him Jesus. Then, this child will be great. He will be called Son of the Most High. He will be given the throne of David. He will rule over the house of Jacob. His reign will have no end.

Mary has good reason to be afraid, and not just because of the awesome, terrifying apparition. Now she is told that she, an unwed woman, will become pregnant. If this news got out, she could be legally stoned to death on the spot.

She is afraid, but told not to be afraid. As she hears this news, she becomes confused. "How can this be, since I am a virgin?" she asks. She regains her composure, and like Elizabeth's husband Zechariah, boldly questions the angel. In her case, the questions are respected and answered.

In a world where God seems so absent, the angel declares that God is quite present and active. God has decided to do something dramatic, he explains. God will overshadow you, and create a human being through you. Indeed, Mary will give birth to God. This child will become the savior of the world and his reign will last forever. Even Elizabeth who was barren is now expecting a child, the angel continues, "for nothing will be impossible with God."

Two thousand years later it is still hard to grasp the message of the angel, much less the events which unfolded. The announcement of the incarnation of God is the greatest event in human history for those who believe it. For Christians, everything is changed: World history has been altered. Life is charged with God's spirit. God has shared our burden and knows our troubles. Anything is possible. There is reason for hope. We are not abandoned.

Each one of us has to grapple with the angel's announcement and how to respond to it. The key to understanding it and accepting it lies in our relationship with God and our understanding of ourselves. If we see our lives in a loving relationship with God and understand ourselves as God's servants and friends, then we can accept this dramatic news with grace. If we do not operate from this loving faith context, then we will be less open to God's loving invitation.

Mary's reaction to this news, beginning with her fear and confusion, springs from her basic humanity and her dependence on God. Fear and confusion are the natural responses to such a supernatural experience. If Mary were not a person of prayer, a person of contemplative peace, a person who shares herself intimately with God, she would run screaming from the house, or dismiss the whole episode as a crazy nightmare or a ridiculous daydream, and we would never have heard of her.

But Mary is secure in herself as God's servant. She seeks intimacy with God. She is a person of contemplative peace. So she accepts the unimaginable with grace. She teaches us that life requires self-knowledge, self-confidence, an intimate loving relationship with God and trust in God. From this contemplative peace, anything is possible, even our acceptance of God's will.

I have never seen an angel, heard the voice of God or witnessed an apparition, but I have been afraid and even terrified. Though I'm a broken, sinful man, I try to meditate regularly in a spirit of contemplative nonviolence. I always feel better afterward. More often than not, the rhythm of prayer and my encounter with God in prayer moves me from desolation to consolation, from fear to joy, from confusion to trust, from anguish to peace, from feeling alone and unloved to feeling

God's presence and overwhelming love. That in itself is a miracle!

Over time, I have begun to understand life as a journey in relationship to God. As I take time to sit in that relationship each day, I learn to feel God's intimate presence. Over many years, this life of contemplative prayer has been a continuing unfolding of self-knowledge, a shocking growing awareness of my brokenness, my dependence on God and God's unending kindness. It is not that I have stopped being a sinner; I am still a sinner. It is that God has never stopped loving me, forgiving me, and pouring out mercy upon me. God has never failed me. The ever-growing awareness of my frailty and need for God is a great gift, perhaps the greatest lesson in life. It will continue to grow until the hour of death.

Prayer is the journey into that mystery of mercy and dependence. The growing awareness of this need for God leads us back again and again to wait for God. In the end, life becomes one long "waiting on the Lord," as the psalmist writes and the saints testify. One finds oneself falling in love with God, and then waiting for God. The process of loving dependence and expectation for God opens our hearts and leads us to seek God in those around us and in the whole human race. This journey into God takes us into loving service of others. Along the way, we grow in humility, without even knowing it. We begin to sacrifice ourselves for those in need. And we delve deeper into the spirit of peace.

Mary somehow learned this contemplative rhythm early on. She waited for God, opened herself to God, and gave herself to God. Then, one day, God came to her. God decided she was the one to give birth to the messiah. She had waited in peace for the coming of the God of peace, and in the end, gave birth to the God of peace and became the mother of peace.

This great gospel lesson urges us to wait for God, seek God, pray for God's peace, plumb the depths of contemplative peace, and open ourselves to the unimaginable appearance of the God of peace. Mary's encounter with God invites *us* into an encounter with God. If we dare enter into God's contemplative peace, then perhaps, like Mary, we too will see the vision of God and hear God's loving invitation.

Someday, when we least expect it, God will show up. According to the scriptures, that day is coming. It may be tomorrow, fifty years from now, or at the hour of our death. But sooner or later, we will stand before God and know the fear and confusion of Mary. If we begin the journey of contemplative peace now, we will also know the joy and peace which Mary knew as she said "Yes."

THREE

Behold the Servant
of the God of Peace

"Behold, I am the servant of God," Mary tells the angel. "Let it be with me according to your word."

With that yes, the story of Jesus begins. God becomes human. We humans learn first hand about God. Everything can change for the better, if we only heed the invitation.

But Mary's yes could not have been easy. Even though she is a young, frightened girl, there must have been a hard-fought inner life of prayer and peacemaking for her to move from fear and confusion to humble acceptance of God's will. According to various scripture scholars, including a leading feminist theologian, a better translation of Mary's answer would be, "Behold, I am the slave of God." The Greek word implies that Mary sees herself not just as a servant, but as God's slave. In this politically incorrect description, Mary obeys the orders of her master. As a slave, she has no real personal life; she suffers by doing whatever the master requires of her. Her obedience is complete. There is no other alternative.

The saints of history, from Paul of Tarsus to Dorothy Day, testify that real obedience to God leads to redemptive suffering and love, and from there, to the mystical experience of freedom. The "slave's obedience" to God somehow is not violent, but in the end, life-giving, liberating, transforming, leading to the depths of love and peace. Obedience to God leads ultimately to joy because it leads to God.

In Mary's obedience to God we see the deep love of consent. "Let it be done to me," Mary declares. Mary knows that choosing what God wants is always right, even if it does not make sense at the moment.

Mary's yes comes because she has dedicated herself to God. She has spent herself contemplating God and preparing to obey God. Because God holds the exclusive priority in her life, she understands herself in relation to God. She knows herself as servant and slave of God. She waits day and night to do God's will. This loving obedience is the purpose of her life.

But the mystery of God's love leads to another unexpected outcome. Because Mary is so faithful, devoted, obedient, and centered on God, she is treated by our loving, gentle God not as a slave, but as "the favored one." She is hailed by God's messenger and becomes "the mother of God." God treats her not as a brutal, domineering slave master—because God cannot be brutal, domineering, violent, or oppressive—but with compassion and love.

Mary's choice for God was right. It was difficult but beautiful as any choice for goodness, for God, for life must be in such a world. And Mary keeps her end of the bargain. She is faithful to her identity as God's servant. In the end, she stands at the cross of her crucified son, and sits with his friends when his Holy Spirit descends upon them at Pentecost. She remains lovingly obedient because she is devoted exclusively to God. She knows who she is. She knows her true self because she sees herself always before God.

The self-understanding that flows from one's loving relationship with God is the essence of the spiritual life. Thomas Merton called prayerful self-knowledge the movement from the false self to the true self. We live our lives lost in a wide array of illusions, based on negative childhood experiences and the violence and empty promises of the culture. The journey from illusion to reality and our real identities occurs in our prayer journey of loving intimacy with God. Through contemplative prayer, Merton taught, we see our false illusions for what they are and also catch a glimpse of our true selves. In the light and grace of God, we see who we can be, who we are meant to be, who we are invited to become, the people deep down who we already are. Through contemplative prayer, we grow into becoming the people God created us to be, God's own loving sons and daughters, living in devotion to God, seeking to do God's will, trying to reflect God's compassion to all other people, God's other sons and daughters. The journey of life and the road to peace take off from this contemplative acceptance of our true identities, our true selves, our right understanding of ourselves as God's servants, slaves, children, and friends.

When I reflect on this scene between Mary and the angel and measure my life beside it, I nearly despair to realize how far I am from such radical devotion to God. For years, I have struggled not to serve the false gods of war and hatred. I have tried to serve the living God, and so to resist the false gods of war. But have I responded obediently to God's invitation, God's mission of love, God's gift of peace? Alas, no. I continue to resist God, to cling to my false self, to pursue selfish ways, to assert my will, to do what I think needs to be done. Worse, I pretend to myself that I have achieved (by my own merit) the grace of God, and find myself subconsciously filled with pride and self-righteousness, like a modern-day Pharisee. I fall far from the humble devotion portrayed by Mary in the story of the Annunciation. Instead of progressing, I consistently regress further into sin and selfishness. I continue to live out of my false self image, instead of claiming my true self as the son of the God of peace. This orientation of selfishness leads me into trouble time and time again. I think I am free, but in fact, I am a slave to sin, captive to the world. If I sought to be an obedient slave of God, like Mary, then perhaps I would actually enter true spiritual freedom and be liberated from the world of violence.

Mary's acceptance of God's will challenges me on a variety of levels. Do I wait upon God day after day? Can I live as a humble slave of God, trying to do only God's will and not my own selfish will? Dare I let go of my false self? Do I want to see God? Would I truly want to join God's salvific work? Can I accept the life of holy obedience to God and live in the freedom of God's grace? Will I become the person God intended me to be; God's loving, compassionate, peacemaking son? Dare I choose to be chosen by God? Can I ever say with Mary, "I am the servant of the God of peace; let God's will for me be done"?

Mary's example challenges me but also encourages me. It invites me to pursue God through intimate prayer and humble obedience. It summons me to the depths of contemplative nonviolence, to the God of peace. Though I am not yet God's faithful servant and friend, I desire to become so, and pray for the desire and reality of my conversion toward my true self as God's servant, friend, and son. Mary gives me hope that nothing is impossible with God, that even I, a sinner and Pharisee, can be transformed by God's grace into God's servant, God's son, God's peacemaker, God's friend. With Mary, I can ask for the gift and try to live as if it has already been given because in fact it has. The more I live as God's servant, the more I humble myself before God, the more I can cooperate with God's liberating grace and be transformed here and now into God's peacemaker. In this contemplative process, God may use me to serve God's peace, in some way that I may not understand and never understand in this life. In the end, becoming God's servant and friend is a pure gift. There is nothing I can do to earn it; all I can do is accept it humbly with gratitude as a gift given over and over again. Perhaps that is all that is required of us.

I write this on Block Island, Rhode Island, during a cold January storm. I have spent the day walking along the breaking waves at the foot of the eroding Mohegan cliffs under the watchful eye of several large seagulls. This morning, I saw for the first time a whale swimming in the ocean, not far out from the town harbor. Every few seconds its spout let out a burst of water. Then it rolled gently along the ocean surface and back down into the sea. It has been a quiet day, a day of peace.

I look at the sky, the ocean, the cliffs, the birds, the rocks and wonder, "What would it mean for me to change? How can I undergo an inner renewal, a true conversion of heart, and transformation of spirit, so that like Mary, I can respond to the grace of God, become my true self, and be God's servant of peace? I have spent years in pursuit of the gospel call to make peace and seek justice, working in soup kitchens and homeless shelters, teaching high school and college students, living in El Salvador and Northern Ireland, demonstrating against war and nuclear weapons, studying philosophy and theology, lecturing on disarmament and social justice, leading retreats on Christian nonviolence, and going to jail for nonviolent civil disobedience. I have lived in Jesuit community, attended regular eucharist and bible studies, made annual retreats and periodic thirty-day retreats, and seen a spiritual director almost monthly since 1982. But nothing I can do will make me God's faithful servant. I fall far short of the goal. All I can do is beg God to have mercy on me. The only option left is to pray non-stop for my conversion and transformation. Through it all, God remains faithful to me. God takes pity on me, and invites me over and over again into God's life of peace. God summons me to an inner change that will lead me deeper into God's own peace.

As God's servant, at some point, Mary let go of her personal ambitions and selfish desires and focused solely on God. She accepted her human poverty and powerlessness and placed herself completely at God's disposal. God responded dramatically. Because she knew who she was, because she let go of her false self's illusions and accepted her true self as God's servant, she was ready to accept God's will. Her yes to God is the fruit of contemplative prayer. It is the yes of a peacemaker, of a daughter of God.

The best way to prepare for God's sudden and surprising appearance and our affirmative response to God's invitation is through regular contemplative prayer. Those who spend their lives in quiet intimate prayer know God. They fall in love with God and like to adore God in peace and quiet. They become "fully known" by God. They grow familiar with God's spirit, feel God's peaceful presence, and live in the shadow of God's love. When the time comes, they respond positively. Like Mary, they declare instinctively, spontaneously, obediently, lovingly, "Let it be with me according to your word."

A legendary story is told among the Jesuits of New Orleans about a charismatic priest, C. J. McNaspy, who died suddenly in 1995 after declaring his acceptance like Mary. C. J. had spent his life teaching students, serving the poor, playing music, writing books, editing articles, and traveling the world. At the age of sixty-five, he moved to Paraguay where he became a missionary and an overnight celebrity as a church historian and social commentator. In the late 1980s and early 1990s, he was back home in New Orleans, living in the Loyola University Jesuit Community, writing his autobiography and undergoing treatment for cancer.

One Sunday afternoon, he was lying in bed listening to a Beethoven symphony with a friend when something extraordinary happened. The music had just ended, and the friend stood up to put on some Mozart. As the friend turned his back, C. J. jumped straight up in bed, shouted out "Yes! Yes! Yes!" and then fell back, dead.

Later everyone assumed that God had appeared to him and asked him if he would like to come to heaven. Like Mary, C. J. was ready and answered affirmatively.

Mary's yes was the fruit of prayer, self-abnegation, and humble obedience to God. Jesus must have learned these holy attributes from his mother. He too practiced contemplative prayer, self-denial, and humble obedience before God. He understood himself as the servant and slave of God. Then one day, he heard God address him as God's "favored one," "my beloved," "my son." When the hour came for him to be arrested and led to his death, he prayed like Mary to do God's will. In the Garden of Gethsemane, Jesus offered God the same holy obedience he learned from his mother. "Let not my will, but yours be done," he prayed. Luke records that the angels came and comforted him.

Jesus learned like Mary that a full yes to God does not come cheap. It cost her and it cost him.

Jesus may have realized from his mother that true fidelity to God comes at a price. It requires sacrifice, selflessness, surrender, suffering, even death on a cross. But it always leads to eternal life with God.

Mary's yes, like Jesus' later yes, was revolutionary. In a world of imperial politics, militarism, poverty, and executions, it could only mean trouble. She had good reason to be afraid, yet she accepted God's word, come what may. She would do whatever God wanted. She was not the servant of Caesar or Herod. She was the servant of God.

At this point in Luke, we still know very little about Mary, so we don't know her level of awareness of the political ramifications of her response to God's invitation. Later, in the Magnificat, we will see that Mary knows all too well the revolution her yes entails. I believe Mary was politically aware and socially critical of her imperial world because as a poor country woman in the outskirts of an empire, she could have no other perspective. I believe Mary resembles the many struggling, oppressed women I met in the countryside of war-torn El Salvador during the 1980s. These women had nothing, except their dignity, their spirits, their determination, and their trust in God. They knew full well the deadly impact of the Salvadoran military, U.S. military aid, first world consumerism, third world poverty, and war. They were politically astute and biblically literate. Mary would have been the same.

When the angel told Mary about a reign that will never end, Mary would have compared it to the oppressive Roman empire and the emperor who ordered that he be worshipped as god. Mary's acceptance of God's message and the coming of a savior with a reign that would never end meant that she would confront the Roman empire head on, and in effect, overthrow it. Because she longs for liberation from this brutal empire, its idolatrous leader, and his never-ending wars, she accepts her mission. She sees that God is leading a nonviolent social, political, economic, and spiritual revolution. Mary sees herself as God's servant and thus also as the servant of God's nonviolent revolution. Her yes was itself an act of nonviolent resistance to the Roman empire, and a step toward the disarmament of the world.

Mary's yes shows that unlike the emperor and his servants, she does not try to play God. She does not worship the emperor or obey the empire. She differs from everyone who wants to be God. For the emperor, being god means dominating humanity, killing your enemies, and controlling the world's poor. Every empire since then seeks global domination and control.

Yet in the Annunciation we read an entirely different scenario. Mary says yes to God because she never claimed to be God or tried to play God or dominate over anyone. She tried to be herself, to be the selfless servant of the true God. Mary tried to be human, and so she could say yes to God and give birth to the divine. Her yes is a gift to the whole human race and gives birth to the model human being who will show us all how to be human.

But the story of the Annunciation reveals something even more astonishing. Just as we want to be divine instead of being human, God wants to become human. God wants to share human life and show us in the process how to be human. The implication is clear: we no longer have to play God. All we have to do is be human.

In these inhuman times, it is practically impossible to know how to be human anymore. The higher values of compassion, love, nonviolence, and truth are crushed by violence, war, consumerism, hatred, and lies. Television commercials tell us that to be human, we have to buy a certain product. The government tells us that to be human we have to pay taxes, do what we are told, and not rock the boat. The Pentagon tells us that to be human we have to kill our enemies, who are not human.

Mary is human and says yes to God's desire to become human and share the life of humanity. Her mission is awesome to behold. But the angel does not leave Mary alone without any support. With a touch of "human" kindness, the angel tells Mary that her kinswoman Elizabeth, a holy, devout, and barren woman, is also miraculously pregnant. Mary will find support in this other faithful woman who has been chosen by God to do God's work.

When the angel leaves, Mary packs her bags and "makes haste to Elizabeth." She immediately tries to help out someone in need, a woman six months pregnant. Mary's journey to Elizabeth demonstrates that contemplative nonviolence leads to active nonviolence. Mary's spiritual encounter with God in her prayer pushes her to love her neighbor.

But Mary is no longer afraid. She runs out into the world with a heart full of love. She has become God's peacemaker.

II. THE VISITATION: MARY AND ACTIVE NONVIOLENCE

In those days Mary set out and went with haste to a Judean town in the hill country, where she entered the house of Zechariah and greeted Elizabeth. When Elizabeth heard Mary's greeting, the child leaped in her womb. And Elizabeth was filled with the Holy Spirit and exclaimed with a loud cry, "Blessed are you among women, and blessed is the fruit of your womb. And why has this happened to me, that the mother of my God comes to me? For as soon as I heard the sound of your greeting, the child in my womb leaped for joy. And blessed are you who believed that there would be a fulfillment of what was spoken to you by God."

Luke 1:39-45

ONE

Love Your Neighbor

In the story of the Visitation, Mary responds to her encounter with God by reaching out to help someone in need. She hastens to serve Elizabeth. She moves from contemplative nonviolence to active nonviolence.

As she arrives, Mary greets Elizabeth with the words of peace. She offers the traditional greeting, "Shalom." Elizabeth is filled with consolation, and bursts out with praise for Mary. The women then tell their stories to one another, praise God, and celebrate their miraculous pregnancies with great joy. Mary stays for several months, probably until after Elizabeth's baby is safely delivered.

One way to read the story of the Visitation is to focus on Mary's active nonviolence, in this case, her loving service, affectionate friendship, and community building. Because she put her contemplative nonviolence into action, Mary's spiritual journey moves from her initial fear and confusion in the presence of the angel to consolation and joy in the presence of Elizabeth. Because of Mary's outreach, the pregnant Elizabeth and the unborn John are filled with joy as they recognize the presence of the God of peace. Mary's good deed immediately makes people happy.

Mary's active nonviolence highlights several features of the spiritual life. First, true contemplative nonviolence leads to action on behalf of those in need. Her journey to Elizabeth invites us to turn our contemplative prayer into loving service of others. It asks us to reflect if our contemplative prayer leads us to active outreach to the poor. Gandhi taught that nonviolence "is not just a private matter. It must be practiced." Mary practices nonviolence. If we wish to follow her into the spiritual life, we too need to put our nonviolence into action.

The story of Mary's encounter with the angel and her visitation to her cousin Elizabeth is all too familiar, but two words in the text shake us into realizing how urgent her love was. We are told that Mary set out "with haste." The journey on foot to Elizabeth's home, if she lived in Ein Karim as tradition holds, would have been a dangerous ninety-mile pilgrimage from Nazareth through mountains, desert, woods, soldiers, and robbers. She sets off quickly, like Israel in exile, a scene the entire Holy Family will reprise in their flight from Herod into

Egypt. Mary puts her fears and worries aside to be with her cousin, to assist in her delivery, and to share their amazing experiences with God's angel. Mary does not wait; she takes action immediately. She is a doer.

Mary's active nonviolence teaches us not to wait for someone else to assist a needy person, but to get up and reach out ourselves. It calls us to put our prayer into practice and love the concrete people around us, our neighbors. This love in action was the hallmark of Dorothy Day, founder of the Catholic Worker. After years as a communist, journalist, and agitator, Dorothy moved to a Staten Island cottage along the beach to give birth to her daughter in the late 1920s. For months she walked along the shore. Those contemplative days changed her life. For the first time, she felt the presence of God. She wanted to give thanks, to praise the Creator, to name the peace she experienced. In response, she brought her baby girl to church and had her baptized, and decided to get baptized too.

As a newborn Catholic, Dorothy continued her prayers for peace, her passion for justice, and her service to the homeless. With Peter Maurin, she welcomed homeless people into her apartment, and founded the first of hundreds of Catholic Worker Houses of Hospitality. They housed, fed, served, cleaned, clothed, ministered to, and loved the poor and disenfranchised. They welcomed the poor into their hearts as if they were long lost family members. Together, in a spirit of solidarity they adopted voluntary poverty and gave away their own personal money and possessions. They wanted to serve and love Christ present in the poor. Every arrival of a person at their door was another reenactment of the visitation.

For Dorothy, active nonviolence is the flip side of contemplative nonviolence. She insisted on the Church's "works of mercy" as well as the works of prayer and the works of justice. She rose at six a.m. each morning for two hours of prayer and bible reading, and then went to morning Mass. Then, she fed the hungry on the soup line, cleaned the dishes, worked on the newspaper, joined a peace protest, or gave a lecture. Dorothy was nonviolence in action. She embodied the story of the Visitation, being good news to the poor people she served. Like Mary, she became a prophet of nonviolence.

There are countless other examples of quiet people giving their time and energy to the suffering poor and homeless. Another example which touches me deeply is the story of Jean Donovan, the twenty-two-year-old Cleveland accountant who felt drawn to the church, who quit her job at Arthur Andersen and moved in the late 1970s to minister to impoverished El Salvador. As the war exploded around them and other missionaries fled, she decided deliberately to stay. She wanted to serve the poor no matter what the cost, even as the war closed tighter around her.

"Several times I have decided to leave," she wrote a friend in late 1980, shortly before she was brutally raped and assassinated along with three North American nuns. "I almost could except for the children, the poor bruised victims of adult lunacy. Who would care for them? Whose heart would be so staunch as to favor the reasonable thing in a sea of their tears and loneliness? Not mine, dear friend, not mine."

Martin Luther King, Jr. described such costly nonviolence as "love in action," using the specific Greek word for love, *agape*, meaning "unconditional sacrifice, all-encompassing love." As Dorothy Day and Jean Donovan lived it, nonviolence meant putting one's own personal needs and wants second, and placing the needs of the poor first. It meant reaching out in love to the poor, even giving one's life to the poor. These women peacemakers knew the beauty and power of Mary's visitation to Elizabeth. In that first act of the gospel they would have found a model of active love, a way to live the spiritual life.

A second lesson of the Visitation is the need to practice active nonviolence toward the people in need around us, beginning with our family and friends. Nonviolence begins at home, with our families, parents, spouses, children, sisters, brothers, and relatives. It means loving-kindness first among those God has put in our life. As we seek to promote peace and show compassion publicly in the world, we need to show compassion and kindness to those in our own lives. Nonviolence demands consistency. It requires love toward everyone. The contemplative peace that comes from prayer and the encounter with God leads us to a new nonviolent attitude toward ourselves and those around us. Then, we can turn to the bigger problems in the world.

Gandhi often told people not to wait for some improbable day when they would meet King George, the imperial ruler over India, to begin the journey of nonviolence. Practice it now, he said, in your families, among your relatives, with your friends, with all those in your immediate circle, especially toward those in need. Start with the people right in front of you. He offered a simple, human teaching, one that Mary modeled.

Mary undertook a concrete act of kindness toward her pregnant, elderly cousin. Active nonviolence deepens family relationships, helps those in need, shares their joys and burdens, and expands the love among us. Mary changed world history, and she did so first through a quiet yes in her contemplative prayer, followed by a quiet visit to her pregnant cousin. Hers was a pure, loving nonviolence, a deep, affectionate kindness to the people around her.

Nowadays, in our busy lives and tumultuous world, with its long history of resentment and violence, we sometimes decide not to help each other out. Mary shows us how to be there for each other. She could have done a million things, including call attention to herself. But she puts her own interests aside. She teaches us to enact our nonviolence by reaching out with genuine human kindness to those in need, beginning with our relatives.

Finally, Mary's active nonviolence builds community. By reaching out to serve someone in need, she deepens the bonds of community. When we reach out in active love to our neighbors in need, we can build community with them, and in the process, create a new pocket of love, care, hospitality, and peace for one another.

"Love comes with community," Dorothy Day wrote in the conclusion of her autobiography, *The Long Loneliness*. She knew the importance of community if we want to be faithful to the life of active nonviolence. Mary learned this too when she gathered with Jesus' friends after his ascension and experienced Pentecost.

"When I am commanded to love," Martin Luther King, Jr. wrote, "I am commanded to restore community, to resist injustice, and to meet the needs of my brothers and sisters."

Nonviolence, King taught, is "love seeking to preserve and create community. It is insistence on community. *Agape* is a willingness to sacrifice in the interest of mutuality. *Agape* is a willingness to go to any length to restore community. It doesn't stop at the first mile, but it goes the second mile to restore community. It is a willingness to forgive, not seven times, but seventy times seven to restore community. The cross is the eternal expression of the length to which God will go in order to restore broken community."

Shortly after the Montgomery Bus Boycott King concluded, "The aftermath of nonviolence is the creation of the Beloved Community while the aftermath of violence is tragic bitterness."

Mary's example invites us to put our contemplative nonviolence into action, and thus to serve the poor, deepen our friendships, and build community. Simply by making haste through the country to visit Elizabeth, Mary shows us concretely how to love those in need; to deepen the key relationships in our lives; to risk our lives if necessary for those in need; and to build community with the people God has given us in our lives.

Mary's visitation to Elizabeth asks us: How do we love our neighbors, serve the poor, and stand with the marginalized? Do we deepen relationships with our relatives and friends and build community with those around us, especially the poor and needy, as we journey on the road to peace? How do we move from fear and confusion to consolation and joy? In other words, do we put our experience of contemplative nonviolence into action by reaching out to those in need?

In the months that followed the September 11th attacks, thousands of New Yorkers began to visit those in need, offer support, and practice compassion on a wide scale. I witnessed many acts of kindness at the Family Assistance Center, the main headquarters for those who lost loved ones at the World Trade Center. Thousands of volunteers assisted the grieving and needy. Tons of food, clothing, medical, and financial donations were offered. Millions of cards and letters poured in from around the country.

Some women who lost loved ones in New York and Washington, D.C. flew to Afghanistan under the auspices of Global Exchange, a non-profit social justice organization, and met with relatives who lost loved ones in the U.S. bombing of Kabul. They embraced widows, wept together, forgave one another, held traumatized children, and offered each other the gift of peace and love. These women embodied the story of the Visitation. They took Jesus' commandment to love our neighbors one step further, as Jesus instructed, and loved their country's enemies. They demonstrated the full length and breadth of active nonviolence. They show us that the whole human race is in fact one family, that we are one world, that we are all united in a common bond of love. Such acts of nonviolent love sow the seeds of healing and peace. They also lead to a prophetic call for peace and justice.

TWO

The Words of Peace

When Mary reaches Elizabeth, the first thing she does is offer the greeting of peace. What does Mary say? She would have called out to Elizabeth with the word, "Shalom!" "Peace!" This greeting of peace sets the whole encounter in motion. Elizabeth's unborn child jumps for joy. Elizabeth bursts out with exuberant praise of Mary and God. Filled with joy, Mary too starts praising God and proclaiming God's reign of justice and peace.

I believe that Jesus learned much about nonviolence and love from his mother. Surely, he would have greeted his disciples and friends with the same greeting of peace, and meant it with all his heart. When he finally sent his disciples out into the world to preach about God's reign, he told them that as soon as they arrived in a village, they were to greet everyone with a blessing, saying, "Peace be with you." If you are with peaceful people, they will receive your peace, he said, and you can stay with them in peace. Otherwise, you should leave them. After Jesus was executed and rose from the dead, Jesus' first words to his frightened disciples was this same greeting of peace, which he learned from his mother. "Peace be with you," the risen Jesus said to his disciples. After showing them his wounds, he repeated his greeting, "Peace be with you!" Once again, people were filled with joy and consolation.

Since the Second Vatican Council, the greeting of peace has become a central experience of the eucharist. Before receiving Holy Communion, everyone is invited to turn to those near them and bless them with the words, "The Peace of Christ be with you." Those words of blessing and reconciliation may be the most important change in modern Catholic history. If Christians begin to live out the meaning of these words, then the peace of Christ will take deeper root among us. We will refuse to kill one another or wage war because the peace of Jesus will rule our hearts.

In my Jesuit community, we have a tradition for the sign of peace. At our liturgies, instead of standing, shaking hands or embracing one another, we usually push our chairs together in a close circle, join hands, look at one another, smile, and say in unison, "Peace of Christ be with you." In that greeting of Christ's peace, we form a community of the heart, and the spirit of peace deepens among us. It is a small and quiet event, totally lost upon the world, but it regularly heals and transforms us.

It seems so basic, but in these times of global terrorism, nuclear weapons, and widespread violence, the language of nonviolence is still critically important. If we want to live in peace with one another, we need to reject the language of violence and speak the words of peace to one another.

Thich Nhat Hanh advises us to be mindful about every word that we speak to another person. If we use language that does not hurt people but that affirms people, we will lead people to greater peace, happiness, hope, and consolation. If we use the language of violence and fear, we will speed up the culture's downward spiral. There is much more than language in the life of active nonviolence to be sure, but the word is a powerful weapon. Indeed, John's gospel testifies that Jesus embodies the Word of God. He used only words of peace, that is, he spoke the truth with love. He spoke of nonviolence and the God of peace. He rarely shared his fears, anger, disappointments, resentments, and bitterness. He used words that healed, helped, affirmed, disarmed, and loved. His words served those around him, and continue to bear good fruit. Two thousand years later, we remember his words of peace. His speech continues to transform the world.

We too need to use nonviolent language with one another, beginning with our spouses, parents, sisters and brothers, children, relatives, friends, and community members. That may mean learning not to use certain familiar phrases and language, especially the expressions and tones that breed cynicism, despair, resentment, anger, bitterness, or pain.

When Muriel Lester, the British pacifist and founder of London's Kingsley Hall, first visited Gandhi's ashram in the early 1920s, community members told her that after years of practicing nonviolence, they discovered that it was not enough to disarm the body. "We have to disarm the mind as well," they said. "When we do this, when all bitterness and malice are rooted out, when all self-pity, hatred, and jealousy are destroyed, then we are set free." She was greatly impressed by the depth of their nonviolence. Not only were they permanently, physically disarmed—even as they engaged in revolution—but their minds, hearts, and tongues were disarmed as well. They welcomed her, "their enemy," with the greetings of peace. When Gandhi later stayed with her during the 1932 Round Table Conference in London, he too experienced the greetings of peace by everyone. After his three-month stay, he wrote in the Kingsley Hall guest book, "Love surrounded me here."

Mary and Elizabeth stood before each other and exchanged greetings of peace with disarmed hearts and minds. God's gift of peace filled them with joy. They immediately started to share their experience of God, which led to great consolation. Here is a simple but important lesson from these two holy women. We too need to share our experience of God with one another. This exchange will lead us to joy and consolation. If we dare tell one another the good things that God is doing in our hearts and lives, and do so with the language of peace and nonviolence, we will move from fear and confusion to a joy and consolation we had not previously known.

A Jesuit friend and scholar tells of meeting Dorothy Day in the early 1960s when she visited the Jesuit school of theology in Maryland. Only fifteen Jesuits gathered to welcome her and hear her reflections. "What did she talk about?" I asked him. "I don't remember any of it," he said, "except for one thing, which I never forgot. Certainly she must have talked about the Catholic Worker and her hospitality to the poor, but someone asked her to tell them how she survived her many disappointments and problems with the church authorities. 'Oh I never talk about my disappointments,' she answered. I thought that was the most remarkable thing," the Jesuit said. "I was amazed at her. She simply refused to speak negatively about the church or others. She wanted to use the precious time she had to talk solely about the good works they were doing, their pursuit of disarmament, their work to enact the gospel, and the presence of Christ in their midst. That was enough for her, and a great lesson for us."

As I shared these thoughts at the Advent retreat in Pennsylvania, one woman raised her hand and said, "Women have been sharing their stories with one another for thousands of year." Yes, women show us all how to practice peace. But I think Mary and Elizabeth enter not just into conversation, but into "spiritual conversation." Their exchange is full of blessings, praise, God's name, and ultimately the Magnificat. They discuss God's active presence in their lives and it is that God-talk which makes all the difference. Do we engage in heartfelt "spiritual conversation" with one another? It is a great act of faith, hope, and consolation to do so. The act of articulating our experience of God to one another can unleash the springs of contemplative peace within us.

The art of spiritual conversation is one of the hallmarks of Ignatian spirituality. St. Ignatius sent new Jesuits out each day in groups of three to talk about God for a half hour. In this way, they learned not only how to articulate their experience of the spiritual life, but their own spirits were lifted and they were moved to gratitude. St. Ignatius taught that sharing with one another, not just our burdens and difficulties, but the graces that God is giving us will not only help us understand where God is in our lives, but will build community among us and deepen our friendships. These relationships will deepen because they will be rooted in the presence and action of God. They become transformed and sanctified. God builds community among us. After a lifetime of such spiritual conversation, based on our contemplative prayer and love for one another, we become not just each other's friends, but friends of God, members of God's community.

Speaking words of peace to one another can lead us beyond the problems of our personal lives and our world to God. These words of peace will encourage us to take another step together on our journey to God. In our day and age, it is more and more difficult to speak these words and enter into spiritual conversation with one another. If we do, however, we too, like Elizabeth, Mary, and the unborn child, will rejoice and give God thanks. We will sing God's praise and bless everyone we meet with God's shalom.

THREE

Beatitudes of Peace

After Mary's greeting of peace, Elizabeth bursts forth with joy. She welcomes Mary and starts showering her with an array of blessings. Mary's greeting sets off a remarkable conversation that begins with Elizabeth's beatitudes and concludes with Mary's Magnificat.

Luke begins his gospel with the story of the angel's visit to Elizabeth and Zechariah. Though Elizabeth is elderly and childless, she is told she will give birth to a boy whom they must name John. Compared to Mary's story, we are given many more details about Zechariah and Elizabeth. Zechariah objects to the whole possibility as preposterous, and is struck dumb on the spot. Meanwhile, Elizabeth is described as "holy," which is a rare and extraordinary occurrence in the gospels. We know that Elizabeth is a unique and saintly woman. Just being in Elizabeth's presence is a grace and a blessing.

Mary's greeting causes Elizabeth's unborn child to leap for joy in her womb. Elizabeth is "filled with the Holy Spirit," we are told, and cries out in a loud voice. She proclaims three beatitudes, the first of many in Luke's gospel. "Blessed are you among women and blessed is the fruit of your womb," she exclaims to Mary. Then she asks Mary, "And why has this happened to me, that the mother of my God comes to me? For as soon as I heard the sound of your greeting, the child in my womb leaped for joy. And blessed are you who believed that there would be a fulfillment of what was spoken to you by God."

Jesus is known for extraordinary sayings. Most striking are his Beatitudes. Jesus blesses those whom the culture normally curses, the poor, the marginalized, the mournful, the peacemakers, the troublemakers. But the gospels are full of other blessings. Perhaps Jesus learned to pronounce his beautiful Beatitudes from the great women in his life, Elizabeth and Mary. Mary has greeted Elizabeth with the blessing, "Peace be with you," and Elizabeth cries out, "Blessed are you among women." She must have already heard from Mary what had happened, or the angel Gabriel told Elizabeth the news of the coming of the Messiah to Mary.

Elizabeth could have said so many different things to Mary. She could have ignored Mary's greeting, complained of her own pregnancy, exploded at Mary with anger for showing up unannounced or even thrown her into despair over the whole ordeal and suggested an abortion. But Elizabeth is holy, which means she is a woman of prayer and contemplative nonviolence. She already sees how wonderful Mary is in the eyes of God and human history. She declares that Mary is blessed among all women.

In her second beatitude, Elizabeth blesses the child in Mary's womb. Already, Elizabeth believes in Jesus as the Christ whose reign of peace will have no end. Elizabeth is a faithful disciple from the moment of Mary's greeting of peace. Later people will curse Jesus, plot his death, call for his crucifixion and cheer on his execution. Here the first great women in his life bless him and praise him. No wonder God came to these two noble women! They teach us how to be disciples, by loving and blessing Jesus unconditionally with all our hearts. They show us how to be Jesus' friends, sisters, and brothers, like his own intimate family members, which he insists we are.

Have I ever called anyone blessed? I try in my letters to bless my family, friends, and brother Jesuits, but I rarely tell people they are blessed. It is my loss. What a gift to call someone blessed! It is a good practice of interpersonal, loving nonviolence to bless those around us as beloved by God.

One reason Elizabeth cries out her blessings is that her unborn child, who will grow up to become John the Baptist, whom Jesus will call "the greatest human being born of woman," leaps for joy in her womb. John rejoices at the greeting of peace. He already recognizes peace and the God of peace even before he is born. He feels the presence of Jesus, and he leaps for joy. He invites us to rejoice at the greeting of peace, the visitation of Mary, the coming of Jesus in our lives. Our active nonviolence should lead others to rejoice in the God of peace and in the presence of the peacemaking Jesus. John the Baptist learned this early on.

Elizabeth then questions Mary, wondering what makes her worthy to receive a visit from the "mother of my God." Her question significantly names Mary as "the mother of my God," and then turns to ponder Elizabeth's own identity. Just as Mary knew who she was, "the servant of God," her presence forces Elizabeth to search for her own true self. Is she also a servant of God? How is it that she, a poor elderly woman, should be visited by the mother of God? The question reveals Elizabeth's faith, hope, and love. Once again, the presence of God in our midst raises eternal questions about the meaning of life. If we can claim our true identities as God's sons and daughters, God's servants and friends, we will be able to rejoice spontaneously when God shows up at our doorstep.

Questions are important in the gospels. Jesus asks 307 questions (I counted them once). Elizabeth's question and her beatitudes lead Mary to proclaim God's praises in the Magnificat. Likewise, we can ask, "Who are we that God should come to us, that the mother of the Lord should take note of us, that the spirit of Jesus should dwell within us, that Jesus himself should become our food and drink?" One could go on and on with such questions about God's generosity in light of our unworthiness. Such questions lead us deeper into the mystery of life and the gospel pronouncement that God is a gentle loving parent who calls us God's very own beloved sons and daughters.

Elizabeth does not answer her question, nor does Mary. Instead Elizabeth offers a third beatitude. She proclaims Mary is blessed because Mary trusted that God's words would be fulfilled in her. She lifts up Mary's deep trust in God. This beatitude invites us likewise to trust that God's word to us will be fulfilled as well. It summons us to take God at God's word. Later when Jesus calls us to love one another, love our enemies, put down our swords, and even forgive one another, we will be called again to a new level of trust. Mary shows us how to trust God, and Elizabeth helps us by affirming Mary's act of trust. She observes that trust is an act of holiness. To trust God is to be blessed with peace.

Three beatitudes! Both women are brimming
with joy. They are filled with the Holy Spirit and
deeply consoled. St. Ignatius said the whole point
of the spiritual life is to move deeper into the consolation of the Spirit's presence. He advises us to
discern the spirits and follow wherever God's consolation leads us. If we pray regularly and practice
contemplative nonviolence, then engage in active
nonviolence by loving our neighbors in need, we
will find consolation. We too will move from fear
and confusion to joy and peace. We too, like Mary
and Elizabeth, will feel blessed.

III. THE MAGNIFICAT: MARY AND PROPHETIC NONVIOLENCE

And Mary said, "My soul proclaims the greatness of God; my spirit rejoices in God my savior. For God has looked upon God's handmaid's lowliness; from now on all generations will call me blessed. The Mighty One has done great things for me, and holy is God's name. God's mercy is from age to age to those who fear God. God has shown the strength of his arm, and has scattered the arrogant of mind and heart. God has thrown down the rulers from their thrones and lifted up the lowly. The hungry, God has filled with good things; the rich, God has sent away empty. God has helped Israel his servant, remembering God's mercy, according to God's promise to our ancestors, to Abraham and Sarah and their descendants forever."

based on Luke 1:46-55

ONE

My Spirit Rejoices:
God's Revolution
Has Begun

With the Magnificat, Mary makes the jump from active nonviolence to prophetic nonviolence. With joy and unbounded confidence, she announces God's reign of peace and justice, and denounces the world's reign of war and injustice. She not only sums up the message of the prophets but becomes a prophet herself and reveals herself as Jesus' teacher. In the process, she becomes ours, too.

Mary's Magnificat is not just a hymn of praise to God. It is that and much more, a manifesto of revolutionary nonviolence and a call, not to arms, but to disarmament and justice. Before Elizabeth and the soon-to-be-born John the Baptist, she publicly proclaims what God is doing in the world—bringing justice to the poor, fulfilling his promise of peace. She testifies that God is a God of mercy, a God of nonviolence, a God of peace. She tells us that God is doing something great, something unparalleled in human history, by coming to her, a poor, unwed Jewish woman on the outskirts of the Roman empire. She explains that God's mercy and nonviolence act throughout human history, up to and including today. Her proclamation is a prophet's denunciation and annunciation, a visitation of the word of God itself.

Mary is not a passive saint. A contemplative and an activist, a mystic and a revolutionary, Mary is the mother of God and so she boldly proclaims God's word of nonviolence to the world of violence, God's revolution of justice to the world of injustice. She is blatantly political. She does not just rock the boat or shake up the status quo. She turns over the tables of the culture. Mary is dangerous. She disturbs the culture's complacency and stirs up trouble. From the perspective of the rebellious Mary of Nazareth, everything from this point onward is different. Everything is called into question. Everything must change. Yes, she is full of grace, light, love, mercy, and kindness. And she is trouble for every empire, every proponent of violence, every war-maker, every millionaire, every advocate of systemic injustice.

In Mary's day, people were routinely arrested and brutally executed for saying the things Mary declared to Elizabeth. Mary's message is radical revolution, pure and simple: God has thrown down the rulers from their thrones. God has lifted up the lowly. God has filled the hungry with good things. God has sent the rich away empty.

Such serious words cause trouble in our own times, too. Mary's Magnificat was banned in Argentina in the mid-1970s because the Mothers of the Disappeared published it as a call for nonviolent resistance to the military junta. The words are so powerful, they are considered by some to be dangerous.

Mary speaks about political, economic, and social conversion, about nonviolent revolution. She points out God's preferential option for the poor, God's opposition to injustice, and God's faithful commitment to nonviolence and to the community of nonviolence.

For Mary, everything is turned upside-down: all nations, kingdoms, empires, kings, emperors, presidents, prime ministers, billionaires, millionaires, armies, militaries, soldiers, weapons, handguns, bullets, bombs, tanks, nuclear bombs, machine gun buyers-makers-sellers, nuclear weapon manufacturers, crosses, electric chairs, stock exchanges, stock markets, banks, investments, multinational corporations, dictatorships, apartheids, reservations, racisms, slaveries, Klans, segregationists, sexists, elitists, castes, Gestapos, anti-Semites, prejudices, politicians, lawyers, Republicans, Democrats, communists, capitalists, admirals, generals, lieutenants, bombers, Trident submarine commanders, police, jailers, prison guards, executioners, prosecutors, judges, court clerks, lawyers, governors, senators, representatives, mayors, nuclear power plants, nuclear test site officials, scientists, landlords, tax collectors, taxpayers, war-making media anchorpersons, suicidal terrorists, hijackers, kidnappers, rapists, abortionists, animal laboratory scientists, prison contractors, violent revolutionaries, death squads, drug lords, gang murderers, money-worshippers, all oppressive, domineering, religious elites and hierarchies who bless violence with their silence and justify war. All are turned head-over-heels in the upside-down vision of Mary the Mother of God.

Later on, Jesus will pronounce fierce judgments with the same vision of nonviolence, first in his Sermon on the Mount, then in his last words to the community at the Garden of Gethsemane, and from the cross and in his resurrection appearances. Every word he uttered would be a Magnificat of praise to the God of peace and nonviolence and a condemnation of war and violence and their demonic functionaries. "Love your enemies. Hunger and thirst for justice. Forgive seventy times seven times. Put down your sword. Seek first God's reign and God's justice. Peace be with you."

We get a glimpse of Mary's revolutionary non-violence in Dorothy Day, Sojourner Truth, Mother Jones, Kasturbai Gandhi, Elizabeth Ann Seton, Julian of Norwich, Harriet Tubman, Emily Dickinson, Muriel Lester, Rosa Parks, Fannie Lou Hamer, Etty Hillesum, Penny Lernoux, Ita Ford, Jean Donovan, Maura Clarke, and Dorothy Kazel. She is like the mother of Martin Luther King, Jr., who was assassinated while playing the organ during Sunday morning church services at the Ebenezer Baptist Church in the early 1970s. She is like the mother of Steve Biko, who never knew where Steve was, who agonized when he disappeared, and mourned when his broken body was handed over to her. She is like the Mothers of the Disappeared in Argentina, El Salvador, and Guatemala. She is like the women of Malawi, Sudan, Palestine, Iraq, holding their dying, starving, starved, dead children. She is like the women of Auschwitz who were shot and killed as they tried to dismantle the women's gas chamber by hand. She is like the "Women in Black" groups who stand on the street corners of Jerusalem every Friday afternoon to protest the Israeli occupation of Palestine. She is like the women of Belfast, the women of Sarajevo, the women of South Africa, the women of Nicaragua, the women of Chile, the women of Palestine, and the women of Afghanistan. In the Annunciation, the Visitation, and the Magnificat, Mary is the model disciple of contemplative, active, and prophetic nonviolence. She is the true revolutionary, announcing the revolution of God. Her proclamation can lead in only one direction, to the foot of the cross, the empty tomb, Pentecost and the God of peace.

Mary said yes to God, assenting to the angel's announcement that she would bear a child named Jesus. Then, she ran to console Elizabeth who was already miraculously six months pregnant. When Elizabeth burst out with three beatitudes praising Mary and her child, Mary could no longer contain herself. She had moved from initial fear and confusion to consolation and joy. This poor, pregnant, unwed Jewish woman, who would become a refugee and the mother of a hunted criminal executed by the Romans, at that moment, burst forth with overwhelming praise for God.

Mary sees the whole picture. Full of faith and hope, she shouts out to Elizabeth and the whole world a song of gladness and revolution: "My soul proclaims the greatness of God. My spirit rejoices in God my savior." These are words of consolation. They are focused on God, God's greatness, and God's saving action. They are also a public proclamation. If we dare follow Mary on the journey from contemplative to active to prophetic nonviolence, a time will come when we too will have to break through the culture's silence and speak out publicly for God, siding with God, proclaiming God's greatness, announcing God's saving action, and denouncing the idolatrous violence that insults, betrays, and blasphemes the God of peace.

With Mary's hymn of praise to the God of nonviolence, Mary has become a prophet of nonviolence. Her example shows us how to be public peacemakers in a world of war. If we dare welcome the Christ of peace, become his disciples and heed his command to love our neighbors and our enemies, we too have to become prophets of nonviolence.

This is only the beginning. Mary explains in no uncertain terms what God has done. God has not gone to the Roman emperor, the high priest, the regional king, the local rebel, or the village rabbi. "God has looked upon the lowliness of God's handmaid," Mary announces. "From now on all generations will call me blessed. The Mighty One has done great things for me."

The God of the Magnificat takes sides with the poor, the oppressed, and the marginalized—individually in Mary, but socially and globally as well, for all the poor throughout history. First, Mary testifies that God has been active in her life. She knows it, sees it, welcomes it, and trusts it. She is the servant of the God of peace and justice. Elizabeth helps Mary by affirming Mary's decision and confirming that Mary is indeed the servant of God. With Elizabeth's confirmation and support, she realizes that she is blessed and that one day, everyone will see what God has done in her.

Everyone will call her blessed and be touched by her grace. For Mary, being God's servant is not about success, power, effectiveness, or relevance. It is about being faithful to God and blessed by God. She allows God to do whatever God wants with her since she is God's servant, even if that unexpectedly means everyone from now on in history will call her blessed.

In his book, *Unexpected News: Reading the Bible with Third World Eyes*, theologian Robert McAfee Brown put it this way, "Mary can hardly believe it: 'God who is mighty has done great things for me'— for *me*, Mary What's-Her-Name from the wrong side of the tracks, the one with no education, no coming-out party, no executive position in the corporate structure of a multinational corporation, the one who is the object of a lot of sly talk and gossip ('Impregnated by the Holy Spirit indeed! A likely story ...') If this is the way God operates, all bets are off. Our assessment of who is important must be put on hold" (Westminster Press, Philadelphia, 1984, p. 78).

But Mary does not stop there. She goes on to exclaim that what God has done and is doing for her, God does for *all* poor people! Mary announces that God takes the side of *all* the poor and lowly people throughout the world and throughout the history of the world. God shows a preferential option for the poor, the oppressed, and justice. God is not neutral. God is political, social, radical and revolutionary too, and God's revolution is a revolution of nonviolence, liberation, disarmament, and justice for the poor.

Brace yourselves, Mary says to the rich. The time has come for the hungry to be fed, the oppressed to be liberated, the homeless to be housed, the imprisoned to be released, the sick to be healed, the refugee to be welcomed, the marginalized to be cared for, and the poor to be made rich. From now on, everything is changed. God's reign of nonviolence is at hand.

TWO

God's Nonviolence
at Work in the World

For thousands of years, rulers and war-makers have taught us that God is a god of war, a god of violence, a god of wrath, a god who kills, a god who justifies war, a god of terror, a god of hellfire, a god of damnation, a god of condemnation, a god of injustice, a god who prefers the rich, a god who hates the weak, a god who ignores the poor, a god who imprisons people, a god who disregards human suffering, a god of death, a god of evil, a god of nuclear weapons, a god of nuclear war, a god of silence in the face of the planet's destruction, a do-nothing, sound asleep, apathetic, no-good, dead god.

With two sentences, Mary wipes away these false images of God. She dispels our misguided interpretations. "Holy is God's name," Mary declares. "God's mercy is from age to age to those who fear God."

Mary has spent her life sitting in intimate prayer with the God of peace. She has met God's angel. She was told not to be afraid, that God was coming to save humanity and that her son's reign of peace would have no end. She knows who God is and what God is like.

From her experience of the God of peace, Mary announces the very nature, will, and action of God. She speaks the truth about God and God's loving action in the world. In the process, she becomes God's prophet, one who speaks for God, one who speaks the truth. God is holy, Mary insists. Contrary to what the world of violence holds, that means that God is a God of peace, a God of mercy, a God of reconciliation, a God of compassion, a God of liberation, a God of justice, a God of forgiveness, a God of the poor, a God of life, a God of goodness, a God of nonviolence. Mary's theology subverts the fundamental principles not only of the pagan world, but also of the religious world. Mary knows first hand that God's active nonviolence is at work in the world, even in her, in the middle of nowhere.

What does it mean for Mary to claim that God is holy and that God's mercy is at work from age to age? Holiness for Mary entails all that opposes the world's violence and injustice. It includes perfect peace, everlasting mercy, boundless compassion,

unconditional love, steadfast nonviolence, persistent reconciliation, and the unrelenting goodness
that alone overcomes evil. God's holiness means
that we cannot bless war because God is a God of
peace. God cannot be indifferent or hate-filled
because God is a God of love. God cannot lie
because God is a God of truth. God cannot seek
vengeance because God is a God of compassion.
God cannot retaliate because God is a God of reconciliation. God cannot condone violence or be
violent because God is a God of nonviolence. But
more than that: God is peace. God is love. God is
truth. God is compassion. God is nonviolence.
God is the perfect fullness of merciful, forgiving,
all-embracing, all-encompassing, all-inclusive, suffering redemptive love. And this is just the tip of
the iceberg. God is mysterious and larger in goodness and love than we can imagine. As Thomas
Merton wrote, God is "mercy within mercy within
mercy."

God's mercy touches all humanity throughout
history, Mary explains, disarming our hearts and
our world, transforming humanity into God's sons
and daughters, creating nonviolent people of peace
and love. God is not only merciful to every indi-
vidual human being as God's own beloved son and
daughter; God is pouring out mercy through transforming nonviolence upon entire peoples, nations,
classes, races, and religions, as the scriptures
explain and history reveals. Mary testifies that

God's presence works among all those who work for peace, justice, disarmament, and reconciliation. God supports all movements, communities, and peoples of contemplative, active nonviolence throughout history, known and unknown. This is how God works, through sacrificial love among people who promote peace, justice, and reconciliation anywhere, any time, at any point in history. God is always overcoming our evil with divine goodness.

For years I have been studying the movements of active nonviolence throughout history. Though they are ignored by the mass media, history's movements for nonviolent social change reveal God's presence among us. We can trace the Holy Spirit's divine nonviolence at work bringing down the Roman empire, fueling the growing Franciscan movement's defeat of feudalism in the Middle Ages, the abolitionists' struggle to abolish slavery, India's *satyagraha* campaign for independence from Britain, the U.S. civil rights movement's campaign against racism and segregation, and the growing anti-war and anti-nuclear movements around the world.

When we read history through the eyes of peace, with a hermeneutic of nonviolence, we see how God continues to liberate the oppressed, end wars, bring down empires, feed the hungry, house the homeless, and care for the poor. God's mercy is leading people again and again to beat their swords into plowshares and create more just, more human societies.

Recently, a friend of mine, a South African anti-apartheid activist, told me how amazed he was to see film footage of a secret 1987 meeting between apartheid's Prime Minister P.W. Botha and Nelson Mandela, who was brought from prison to Capetown under heavy police security. Mandela was filmed in the police van saying he would not be humiliated by Botha. When he arrived in the middle of the night at the Capitol Building, Mandela refused to walk into the building. Botha is shown walking out to greet Mandela. It was a turning point in South African history. Botha welcomed Mandela and was humbled in the process. His greeting raised Mandela as an equal in the eyes of white South Africans. In that moment, apartheid was doomed. Botha later asked Mandela what he could do immediately for Mandela. Mandela asked for the immediate release of his two best friends and colleagues who were suffering poor health on Robben Island. To the shock of the security officials, Botha ordered their immediate release.

My South African friend describes that secret meeting with awe in religious terms. That exchange led to Mandela's release, new elections, Mandela's presidency, and the abolition of apartheid. God heard the cries of the oppressed blacks of South Africa and led them to freedom. Looking back now, black South Africans see the mercy of God leading them to democracy and justice in martyrs like Steve Biko, nonviolent demonstrations, and inspiring leaders like Archbishop Desmond Tutu. As they struggle now to fight AIDS, HIV, poverty, and crime, they testify again to the mercy of God at work in their new struggles for life.

If we open our eyes and look at the world, we will see God's mercy and nonviolence at work among us, in the Vietnamese and Nicaraguans who forgive North Americans for their wars; in the family members who lost loved ones in the September 11th attacks who speak out against war and violent retaliation; in the families who lost loved ones to violent crime and murder, who oppose the execution of the murderers and call for the abolition of the death penalty; in the persistent peace activists who walk onto U.S. military bases and nuclear weapons installations and start dismantling these weapons in symbolic "Plowshares" actions calling for nuclear disarmament; and in the thousands who gather each year to call for the closing of the so-called "School of the Americas," the U.S. terrorist training camp for Latin American death squads and soldiers at Fort Benning, Georgia.

Though the times are deeply disturbing, there are signs of hope. As I write, on January 24, 2002, the Pope has gathered over two hundred leaders representing the world's major religions in Assisi, home of St. Francis, for a day of prayer for peace. Surrounded by imams, rabbis, patriarchs, nuns, and monks, John Paul II stood in front of the Basilica of St. Francis and urged religious people everywhere to repudiate violence, especially in light of the September 11th attacks.

We must fend off "the dark clouds of terrorism, hatred, armed conflict, which in these last few months have grown particularly ominous on humanity's horizon," the Pope began. "Whoever uses religion to foment violence contradicts religion's deepest and truest inspiration," he said. It is "essential" that religious people "in the clearest and most radical way repudiate violence," he continued, "all violence, starting with the violence that seeks to clothe itself in religion. There is no religious goal which can possibly justify the use of violence by people against people," he concluded.

Such a gathering has only occurred on two other occasions in history, in 1986, in a day of prayer for nuclear disarmament, and in 1993, in a prayer for an end to the Balkans war. Such gatherings offer a hopeful sign of God's mercy working in our time, leading us to a new age of interfaith dialogue, cooperation, nonviolent alternatives to war, and the prophetic call for peace and justice.

Likewise, Mary's proclamation of hope challenges our despair. Her Magnificat directs us to look hard at our lives and our world for the presence of God. Do we see the God at work in history's nonviolent movements against injustice? Do we recognize God's mercy and nonviolence at work today among ordinary people of faith and conscience who struggle against poverty, oppression, injustice, war, terrorism, imperialism, consumerism, and nuclear weapons? Do we believe that God is a God of peace, a God of compassion, a God of justice? Dare we join God's movement of nonviolent transformation, the abolition of war, nuclear weapons, and injustice, once and for all?

Mary invites us to take a leap of faith, like her, to say Yes to God, to trust in God's holiness and mercy, and to recognize God's mercy and nonviolent action at work in our hearts and in our world. The Magnificat calls us to become like Mary, like God, holy, merciful, and nonviolent. Then we too will know better what the holiness of God means, and how God's mercy is at work today healing and reconciling us all.

THREE

The Mighty From
Their Thrones,
the Hungry
Fed and Full

After her proclamation of God's consistent mercy poured out on human history, Mary proceeds to detail God's revolutionary nonviolence with shocking political indictments against the elite and exhilarating hope for the poor. Echoing Hannah's hymn of praise in the book of Samuel (2:1-10), Mary sings about the revolutionary work for justice and peace that God has already done. Through her hymn to the God of justice and peace, Mary blossoms into one of history's greatest prophets of nonviolence.

"God has shown the strength of God's arm," Mary declares. "God has scattered the arrogant of mind and heart." God is active, she insists. God does not hurt or kill anyone, but God scatters the proud, the arrogant, the powerful, the domineering, the oppressive, the violent of mind and heart. God has done this and is doing this right up through today.

"God has thrown down the rulers from their thrones," she continues boldly. This statement is one of the most explosive declarations in the Bible. God does not support any political ruler, any emperor, any king, any president, any prime minister, any general, any secretary of state, any judge, any dictator, any senator, any congressional representative, any principality, any power. God does not condone or bless or even look the other way in the face of domination. God does not just overlook domination. God takes direct, provocative, radical, revolutionary action. God throws these rulers down from their high position of authority and domination over the poor and oppressed.

Although empires, kingdoms, and their rulers seem to last for ages, in fact, according to Mary's declaration, they will all fall. God will throw them down, nonviolently. God has done this in the past with Assyria and Babylonia. God will do this to the Roman empire, and to all empires, dictatorships, and hegemonies to come, from the British empire to the Third Reich, to the dictatorships in El Salvador, Nicaragua, Guatemala, Haiti, and the Philippines, to South Africa's apartheid and the Soviet Union.

But what does Mary's shocking statement mean for the rulers and the mighty of the United States of America? Martin Luther King, Jr. called our country "the greatest purveyor of violence in the world." We can expand that, sadly, to name our country as the greatest practitioner of violence in the history of the world. We are the only ones to use nuclear weapons in war thus far. Our bombs killed over 150,000 human beings in two flashes at Hiroshima and Nagasaki. The innocent life lost is horrifying. The United States ships billions of dollars worth of arms and weapons of mass destruction to over ninety countries each year. It fights in every war in every country; hoards oil and other natural resources all over the planet; finances dictatorships in countries like El Salvador and Guatemala; and trains soldiers at U.S. military schools around the world. Since 1983, the United States has spent over ninety-five billion dollars on missile shield programs to control outer space, which many politicians agree will never work. The United States maintains a global system that helps keep two billion people around the world in poverty, hunger, and misery. Since World War II, we have spent nineteen trillion dollars on war. Fifty percent of every U.S. tax dollar goes to the big business of killing other human beings, while less than fifteen percent pays for development aid for the world's poor.

The Gospel of Luke teaches that God does not tolerate such domination. God will not sit idly by as we decimate entire peoples, whether through bombing raids, nuclear explosions, economic sanctions, or the consumerism and globalization that leads to mass starvation. God has thrown down the mighty from their thrones in the past, according to Mary, and will do so again. We can conclude that God will throw down the mighty in the United States.

Just as God throws the rulers down from their thrones, God also picks up the poor and crushed peoples of the earth. "God has lifted up the lowly," Mary declares. What an astonishing announcement! For the suffering peoples of the earth, there is no better news.

Since World War II, ninety percent of the world's conflicts have taken place in poor countries, according to Caritas-Italy. Since 1945, wars have killed nearly twenty-seven million disenfranchised civilians and produced thirty-five million refugees. Between the years of 1990 and 2000, two million children were killed in war. During the 1990s, there were fifty-six wars in forty-four countries, killing millions of poor people, injuring countless other millions, leaving hundreds of millions permanently scarred by violence. Meanwhile, every day, nearly six thousand people in the world die of AIDS. Twenty million people suffer with

HIV in South Africa. Each month, over five thousand people, mostly children, die in Iraq from economic sanctions imposed by the United States. The list goes on and on.

"All our problems stem from our acceptance of this filthy, rotten system," Dorothy Day said.

Mary's God not only throws down these rulers but actively sides with the poor, with the victims of the first world system, and lifts them up to justice and new life. God picks up those who were pushed down—the homeless, the starving, the refugee, the immigrant, the imprisoned, the sick, the dying, the ostracized, the persecuted. God publicly, actively, politically, socially works to bring them healing, justice, and life. Mary's God comforts the afflicted and afflicts the comfortable, and summons us to do the same.

That any human being is allowed to starve to death is unconscionable, morally unacceptable, sinful, unjust, horrific, and an indictment on us all. Yet every day, sixty thousand people, mostly women and children, die of starvation, adding up to millions each year. Hundreds of millions of people around the world are chronically malnourished. The common experience among human beings today and throughout history has been to live in fear of war, to struggle for food and the necessities of life, and to fall asleep hungry.

To this fourth world of starvation and first world of wealthy oppression, Mary announces,

"God has filled the hungry with good things." Again this is good news for the starving. God is on their side. God has fed people and will feed people. Indeed, as Gandhi once said, in a world of starving people, God comes as our very bread, which God does, in the eucharist. Indeed, Jesus will expand on the Magnificat to declare that whatever we do to the least of these, to the poor, the starving, the homeless, the imprisoned, the sick and the dying, we do to him.

The United States represents only 4.7 percent of the world's population but it controls over fifty percent of the world's resources. We have the power to crush the world's poor or to serve them. God is at work feeding the hungry. We know where we belong: at work with God feeding the hungry.

The flip side of God's feeding the hungry follows next: "God has sent the rich away empty." In order for the hungry to be fed and the poor to have justice, there must be a reversal of fortune. The rich will have to relinquish their money, food, houses, cars, stocks, land, and possessions. According to God's economics, every resource will be shared equally among everyone.

When Mary concludes by pointing out that "God has helped Israel, God's servant," the contrast is equally striking. Of all people to side with! God's support of Israel is as shocking as declaring that God blesses and helps the poorest nations of the world.

The description of Israel as God's servant is equally amazing. As Robert McAfee Brown points out, the master never helps the servant. Servants exist solely to help the master. But here, Mary explains, the roles are reversed. God the master helps Israel the servant. The implication is clear, as Jesus will point out time and time again: if servants are helped, then they are no longer servants. They have become friends and companions. From now on, God serves Israel. Israel has become God's friend.

When Mary praises God for this revolution of justice and peace, she extols not just a new personal morality, but the restructuring of the entire global social order. God is changing not just individuals, but nations, empires, continents, the world, and all generations. God's perspective encompasses every human being who ever lived. At each moment in history, the entire unjust world order is in the process of being toppled over by the God of justice. Though we may not read about it on the front page of the *New York Times*, it is happening at this very moment. The first world media that supports the system of war and corporate greed will never promote the grassroots movement of faith-based revolutionary nonviolence. To find out about it, one has to go to the bottom, into the struggle for justice itself.

"God has remembered God's mercy," Mary concludes, "according to God's promise to our ancestors, to Abraham and Sarah and their descendants forever." With this bold summary, Mary broadcasts to the world that what God promised to Abraham and Sarah has come true, that God has kept God's covenant of peace with humanity in general, and that in particular, God has been faithful to Israel. Her announcement addresses the common doubt of her people. After centuries of oppression, poverty, and suffering under the Romans, the community of faith wondered not only when the messiah would come, but why God had abandoned them. They thought that God had forgotten them. They assumed that God must be like us, forgetful, unfaithful, unreliable, untrue. Because we forget God and our covenant of peace with God, we assume God must, too. It is because we forget God and God's covenant of peace that we forget who we even are and rush off to war.

But Mary has astonishing news: God has not forgotten us! God remembers. God has been faithful to humanity, to God's promise to be with us, and to God's pledge to send us a messiah. Despite our sins, infidelities, violence, injustice and bloodshed, God is still with us. God continues to be merciful to us, just as God promised. God is faithful to us, Mary asserts. "Rejoice with me," she tells Elizabeth. God is coming to us!

The Magnificat sums up the entire gospel. It is a manifesto of prophetic nonviolence calling us to celebrate the God of peace and justice who sides with the poor and liberates the oppressed in their nonviolent struggle for justice. According to Mary, God's transformation of the world has not just begun; it has already happened. God shows a preferential option for the poor; God liberates the oppressed; God topples all ruling authorities and their unjust governments; God lifts up the lowly; God sends the rich away empty; God fills the hungry with good things; God is faithful to God's covenant of peace; God is always merciful to God's people, including and up to this very moment.

Throughout the Gospel of Luke, it can be seen that Jesus learned his revolutionary nonviolence from his mother. He repeats this same call for justice and peace throughout his public life, beginning with his first public sermon in the synagogue of Nazareth (Luke 4). He then goes beyond it in his "Sermon on the Mount," calling us to love our enemies and pray for those who persecute us. He becomes a prophet of nonviolence because Mary was a prophet of nonviolence. Nonviolence is in his blood.

Pondering the extraordinary reversal outlined in the Magnificat, I recall Thomas Merton's brave declaration shortly before his death that he wanted to spend his entire life siding with the poor, the oppressed, the marginalized, the victims of war, the peacemakers, and the persecuted. "It is my intention," Merton wrote, "to make my entire life a rejection of, a protest against, the crimes and injustices of war and political tyranny which threaten to destroy the whole race of humanity and the world. By my monastic life and vows, I am saying NO to all the concentration camps, the aerial bombardments, the staged political trials, the judicial murders, the racial injustices, the nuclear weapons and wars. If I say NO to all these secular forces, I also say YES to all that is good in the world and in humanity." Merton's testimony to peace and justice for the poor continued the tradition of Mary's prophetic nonviolence.

I think too of Martin Luther King, Jr., who more than anyone stands as the prophet of nonviolence for our falling nation. On April 4, 1967, one year to the day before his assassination, King delivered his prophetic speech against the Vietnam War at the Riverside Church in New York City. It was his own Magnificat to the civil rights movement, both exciting and shocking, full of hope and promise and revolutionary challenge.

"I am convinced that if we are to get on the right side of the world revolution, we as a nation must undergo a radical revolution of values," King declared. "We must rapidly begin the shift from a 'thing-oriented' society to a 'person-oriented' society ... A nation that continues year after year to spend more money on military defense than on programs of social uplift is approaching spiritual death. America, the richest and most powerful nation in the world, can well lead the way in this revolution of values. There is nothing, except a tragic death wish, to prevent us from reordering our priorities, so that the pursuit of peace will take precedence over the pursuit of war.

"Our only hope today lies in our ability to recapture the revolutionary spirit and go out into a sometimes hostile world declaring eternal hostility to poverty, racism, and militarism," King concluded. "Now let us rededicate ourselves to the long and bitter—but beautiful—struggle for a new world. This is the calling of the sons and daughters of God, and our brothers and sisters wait eagerly for our response" (James Washington, editor: *A Testament of Hope*, Harper and Row, San Francisco, 1986, 240-243).

On March 31, 1968, just five days before he was killed, King preached his last Sunday sermon at the National Cathedral in Washington, D.C. "America has not met its obligations and its responsibilities to the poor. One day we will have to stand before the God of history and we will talk in terms of things we've done. Yes, we will be able to say we built gargantuan bridges to span the seas, we built gigantic buildings to kiss the skies. Yes, we made our submarines to penetrate oceanic depths. We brought into being many other things with our scientific and technological power. It seems that I can hear the God of history saying, 'That was not enough! I was hungry and you did not feed me. I was naked and you did not clothe me. I was devoid of a decent sanitary house to live in, and you did not provide shelter for me. And consequently, you cannot enter the kingdom of greatness. If you do it to the least of these my sisters and brothers, you do it to me.' That's the question facing America today. I want to say one other challenge that we face is simply that we must find an alternative to war and bloodshed. Anyone who feels that war can solve the social problems facing humanity is sleeping through a revolution. Humanity must put an end to war or war will put an end to humanity" (*A Testament of Hope*, 274-276).

The following Sunday, he was scheduled to preach at his church in Atlanta. The day before his murder, he phoned his Ebenezer Baptist Church from that Memphis hotel room with the title of his upcoming sermon: "Why America May Go to Hell." He never gave it. Like any empire, America cannot tolerate prophets of nonviolence.

Just as Mary became a prophet of nonviolence, so too those of us who follow in her tradition have to become prophets of nonviolence. We have to publicly denounce war and injustice, announce God's reign of peace and justice, and point out God's active nonviolence among us. We have to join it, support it, and give our lives to God's peace movement. Being a servant and friend of the God of peace, Mary attests, means speaking God's word of peace, denouncing our wars and injustices, and announcing God's reign of peace and justice.

Whether our message is well received or not, it must be proclaimed. That is the task before us, to proclaim the truth and live it here and now.

Just as Thomas Merton, Martin Luther King, Jr., and so many others have tried to embody Mary's call for justice, so too the struggling Christian peace movement has tried to put these texts into practice. Years of contemplative and active nonviolence have led us to attempt our own acts of prophetic nonviolence. We too have proclaimed the disruptive, illegal, revolutionary cry of God's transforming nonviolence.

After her Magnificat, Luke reports, "Mary remained with Elizabeth about three months and then returned to her home." She stayed with Elizabeth through the birth of baby John, then journeyed home to prepare for the birth of her child. The story will take off from there, with the Roman census forcing Joseph and Mary to travel to Bethlehem where Jesus will be born into poverty, to Herod's order to kill all newborn boys, their flight to Egypt, the twelve-year-old Jesus' delay in returning to Nazareth as he instructs the high priests in the Temple, to Jesus' dramatic public emergence as a prophet and healer, his civil disobedience in the Jerusalem Temple, and his arrest, torture and execution.

Mary's journey from contemplative nonviolence to active nonviolence to prophetic nonviolence was not easy. She paid a price for her acceptance of

God's mission, her outreach to Elizabeth, her consolation, her judgment on the ruling authorities and their brutal injustices. She taught her son the alternative vision of God's justice, and saw him rejected and brutally killed because of his words of peace by those same imperial forces of injustice and war.

But Mary was right. She was faithful to the God who sent an angel to her. She was faithful to her son. She stood by him in death, would meet him again in resurrection, and share in the Pentecost of his Holy Spirit.

Mary's pilgrimage outlines the journey of nonviolence, from prayer to action to prophecy, and calls us to carry on that same journey, here and now, in our own difficult times.

Conclusion

Mary of Nazareth made the difficult but beautiful journey from contemplative nonviolence to active nonviolence to prophetic nonviolence. She was faithful to the God of peace and the journey to God. She loved God, loved her neighbors and in her prophetic call for justice, loved her enemies. She was a pilgrim of peace, and never turned away from her mission of nonviolence.

As followers of Mary and her son Jesus we too have to start the pilgrimage of peace from contemplative nonviolence to active nonviolence to prophetic nonviolence. In these times of war, nuclear weapons, terrorism, global poverty, corporate greed, executions, and violence, we cannot sit back in silence.

Each one of us has to take up that gospel journey. That means we all have to start anew down the road of nonviolence. We have to turn to God in peace, allow God to disarm our hearts, go forth to our neighbors in need, love our enemies and proclaim God's revolutionary nonviolence to the world. We have to practice Gospel nonviolence, within us, around us, and publicly in our world.

We have to live God's gift of peace in our hearts, practice it among our family, friends, and communities, and proclaim it publicly to the war-making authorities. We have to announce the social, political, and economic consequences of God's reign of justice here and now through steadfast, provocative, prophetic nonviolence, as the epitome of the spiritual life.

Mary's experience at the Annunciation, Visitation, and the proclamation of the Magnificat offers a shining example of committed nonviolence to a world of brutal injustice and war. Her faithful nonviolence gave birth to a nonviolent Messiah who turned over the tables of systemic injustice, suffered martyrdom with love and forgiveness, and rose from the dead to draw all humanity back to God's peace.

Mary hardly makes any other appearance in the gospels after this beautiful portrait in Luke's Gospel. She never says anything else in the gospels, except on two occasions, in the Temple when she asks the twelve-year-old Jesus why he did not return with them (Luke 2:48) and in Cana, at a wedding (John 2:5). When they suddenly run out of wine, Mary informs Jesus and then turns to the servants and says, "Do whatever he tells you."

These words offer a fitting summary of Mary's prophetic nonviolence. She is the favored one of God, the servant of the God of peace, and now has become a disciple of the nonviolent Jesus. Like

John the Baptist, she seeks to "decrease" in order that he may increase. She wants us to do whatever Jesus says.

Mary taught Jesus God's way of revolutionary nonviolence and watched Jesus blossom as the embodiment of God's nonviolence. More than anything, she wants all people to obey Jesus' commandments of nonviolence. Like Jesus, she wants us to love our enemies, pray for our persecutors, forgive seventy times seven times, seek God's reign and God's justice, be as compassionate as God, and put away the sword. She wants us to become, like her, servants of God's peace, disciples of God's peace, mothers, fathers, daughters, sons, brothers, and sisters of God's peace. She wants us to spend our lives practicing nonviolence and making peace as Jesus did.

Two thousand years after Mary's prophetic nonviolence, we have toned down her message and transformed her into someone more manageable, more tolerable, more passive. The culture's false image of Mary does not threaten the status quo. She no longer is portrayed as the model of active and prophetic nonviolence. She is no longer upheld as the spokeswoman of the God of justice, the God of the poor, the God of revolutionary nonviolence. Instead we have set her up on a pedestal where she is safe, far above us, and removed from our troubles. She is stereotyped as a quiet, law-abiding, church-abiding, obedient, subservient woman who does what war-making authorities want. She would hardly recognize herself.

But Luke's portrait remains. Mary's journey sets the whole gospel story of nonviolence in motion. She was filled with joy at God's dramatic entrance into the world, and God's revolutionary action against the rich and powerful and on behalf of the poor and oppressed. Mary understands the plight of all those who suffer from the world's unjust economic order and its wars. She is a woman of justice, a woman of disarmament, a woman of peace, a woman of revolution, a woman of action, a woman of nonviolence.

The nonviolent Jesus and his mother still summon us to the journey of contemplative, active and prophetic nonviolence. In the past, we might have looked to noble heroes like Dorothy Day, Mahatma Gandhi, and Martin Luther King, Jr. for leadership and action. Today, we ourselves have to become heroes, leaders, and saints of active, prophetic nonviolence. We can no longer wait for someone else to make the journey for us. The poor of the earth are dying from our wars and consumerism. The God of peace, the risen Jesus, and his prophetic mother await patiently our response to their invitation, their word, their example.

In the early 1990s, I was privileged to arrange phone conversations for Mother Teresa as she appealed to various governors and judges on behalf of those condemned to die on death row. Two or three times she asked me to recommend one of her favorite prayers to those on death row. "Tell them to pray to Mary with great confidence, saying 'Mary, be my mother now.'"

In our culture of violence, as we carry on the journey of Gospel nonviolence, we have no better model and advocate of Christ's nonviolence than Mary. Mother Teresa's prayer can be our prayer too. If we call on Mary to be our mother, perhaps she will teach us how to become contemplatives, activists, and prophets of nonviolence, and accompany us on the journey ahead to the cross, the resurrection and Pentecost. If we ask her, she will help us become pilgrims and prophets of peace.

All we have to do is ask.

All we need to do is surrender ourselves to the God of peace.

All that is required is to take the next step on the journey of Gospel nonviolence.

© Sally Savage Photography

JOHN DEAR, S.J., is the former executive director of the Fellowship of Reconciliation, the largest inter-faith peace organization in the United States. He is a pastor, community organizer, lecturer, retreat leader, and author/editor of more than twenty books on peace and justice.